MERCHANTMAN? OR SHIP OF WAR

A Synopsis of Laws; U.S. State Department Positions;
and Practices
Which Alter the Peaceful Character of
U.S. Merchant Vessels in Time of War

by Charles Dana Gibson

Published by Ensign Press
P.O. Box 638
Camden, ME 04843
March, 1986

Library of Congress No. 86-80113
ISBN No. 0-9608996-1-8

Dedicated to

The American Mariner
Who Keeps to the Seas in Times of War

ABOUT THE AUTHOR

Charles Dana Gibson is an historian of the war at sea, 1939-45. Gibson is a "hawsepipe" sailor who first went to sea in 1944 at the age of 15. He sat for his 3rd Mates license in 1952 and now holds a Masters license upon Oceans.

Author of THE ORDEAL OF CONVOY NY 119, Gibson is collaborating with his wife in the writing of a 2-volume history of U. S. Army Marine Transportation, 1775-1946.

MERCHANTMAN? OR SHIP OF WAR

TABLE OF CONTENTS

PHOTO SECTION

ACKNOWLEDGEMENTS

The number of people who gave guidance and assistance to me during the process of preparing this work was myriad. I list some of these people below, fully aware that I have probably left out many who deserve inclusion. To those who I have overlooked, I apologize, lamely excusing myself on the basis of a poor memory and my ability to misplace notes.

Foremost, the law firm of Cadwalader, Wickersham, and Taft. An impetus for this book were the words spoken by one of its partners, "the status of the U.S. merchant marine is the one great question remaining unanswered from World War II." The firm generously extended to me the full use of its library which was invaluable in my long quest to answer that question. I especially thank two of the firm's partners, Steve Dune and Jay McDowell who took special interest. I owe a debt to the firm's library staff, Rissa Pecker, John Kruse, and Frank Guglielmo who dug out for me things which were "unfindable."

In the public sector, I was fortunate enough to have the assistance of a variety of archival experts, all of whom either provided source material or leads toward locating same: Dr. Dean Allard, Bernard Cavalcante, Tamara Melia, Nancy Miller, John Reilly, Kathleen Rohr, James Mooney, of the Naval History Division, Department of the Navy; Pat Connell, Jeanette Ford, May Jane Harvey, Joe Swank, Mrs. Love, of the Maritime Administration; Elaine C. Everly, Charles A. Shaughnessy, Michael P. Musick, and Doctor Crawford of the Old Army and Navy Branch, National Archives; Kenneth Hall, Ship Division, National Archives; John Taylor, National Archives; William Sherman, Judicial Fiscal and Social Branch, National Archives; Dee Williams, James Menninger, and Mr. VanDoenoff of the Modern Military Field Branch, National Archives.

Those from the Coast Guard who assisted include: Lt. Garrett, Merchant Marine Inspection Office, Washington; Clint McQuire, International Law Division; Lt. Cmdr. David Wallace, Marine Inspection; and Robert L. Scheina, Historians Office.

Donald Koster and William J. Webb of the Division of Military History, Department of Army; Leslie D. Jensen and Ruth Shepherd of the Army Transportation Museum, Fort Eustis, Virginia; Mrs. Umbrell, U. S. Army Military History Institute; Louise Alder, Desk for Treaty Affairs, Department of State; Robert Laske and Frank Uhlig, NAVAL WAR COLLEGE REVIEW; Vice Admiral R. H. Scarborough, USCG, Retd; Captain Arthur Moore; and Talmadge Simpkins.

To Joan McAvoy who, like myself, has over a period of many months wrestled with the questions at hand: Thank you for your efforts and your critiques.

My gratitude to Rear Admiral Thomas King and Curator Frank Braynard of the U. S. Merchant Marine Academy for their words of wisdom and support.

Most of the photographs in this volume are from the personal collection of Ben Brigadier who took them while in Convoy PQ-18, Iceland to northern Russia, June 1942. During the war, private cameras were prohibited on merchant ships. Unlike the Army and the Navy, the War Shipping Administration sent no official photographers to sea; photographs such as Mr. Brigadier's are almost unknown. I am especially indebted that he shared them for use in this publication.

For their legal guidance, freely offered, without which I might have run astray, I am most greatful to Frank Morrow, Office of the Council, Maritime Administration; and to Captain Harvey Dalton, USN, Office of the Judge Advocate General of the Department of Navy.

Lt. Colonel Michael Dandar, USAF and Lt. Colonel Mary Todd, USAF, of the Civilian/Military Review Board, Department of Defense, were cheerfully forebearing of my innumerable telephone calls to them requesting bits and pieces of information. I thank them for their patience.

To the many ex-Army seamen and merchant seamen whose enthusiasm spurred me on to write this book. This book is especially dedicated to their efforts to gain the recognition they earned. Thank you -- and good luck.

Last and certainly not least, I thank my wife, Kay, that one woman marvel who singulary did the typing of all the drafts, the editing, and the final set up of what you are about to read.

INTRODUCTION

This treatise, as the title would suggest, is an attempt to settle the question, "When is a Merchant Ship No Longer a Merchant Ship?" as that question specifically applies to time of war. I have found, as it pertains to World War II, that there were two answers:

1. The point when a ship becomes joined in the naval war through orders of her government and provided that her crew is under penalty to obey those orders.

2. The point when a ship's activity becomes predominantly one of public purpose in the prosecution of the war, either---

   a. in support of the nation's overall mobilized war effort

   OR

   b. as an auxiliary in direct logistical support of the armed forces.

When these points are taken together, the circumstances, under both law and practice, radically alter the characters of the ship and its crew from that which they held in time of peace.

My purpose here will be to separate out the juridical rulings and legal background, both domestic and international in nature, as well as the historical circumstances which, when taken together, provide the basis through which these transitions take place. As the reader will discover--perhaps to his or her shock--the United States, in World War II, through a process of national control, coupled with military discipline, sent to war thousands of mariners who served under the publicized illusion that they were civilians.

The fact, as this paper will prove, is that those men were actually part of the belligerent armed force. Those men have never received the national recognition due them mainly--I believe, because of the total misinterpretation of their status as it was applicable under both the established Laws of War as well as the statutes of the United States. Hopefully, this treatise will help to provide that proper understanding.

AUTHOR'S NOTE

The primary subject of this work is merchant shipping in time of war. Nevertheless, I found that in the writing it often became necessary to include some discussion of that class of vessel known as auxiliaries of the Army and Navy. This should be of value to the reader as it provides for a separate understanding of the different legal nitch into which naval and military auxiliaries fit. In the case of the world wars, it provides the distinguishing difference between the Army Transport Service (later known as the Transportation Corp - Water Division) and the ships of the merchant marine.

Although not regularly commissioned into the Naval force, auxiliary ships are integrated into their respective Naval or military arm as "public vessels." As such, their normal legal status under both International Law and the U. S. Statutes and Regulations differ in substantial form from that of merchant ships.

Auxiliary ships enjoy the same "sovereign rights" extended under International Law to war ships. The crews of auxiliary ships--although not always themselves members of the uniformed armed forces--are employees of the armed forces, and by that employment, they take on the military character of their ships.

An auxiliary vessel, in the legal sense, retains the same status during war that she possessed during time of peace, except that her function alters from being that of peaceableness to that of belligerency. On the other hand, the status of a merchant ship from peace to war is not a constant thing; rather it is dependent upon the policies of the nation whose flag she flies and the use to which she is put.

LEGAL DEFINITIONS

MARINER: A seaman. A sailor. One who directs or assists in the navigation of a ship. A seafaring man of experience. The technical use of the word "mariner" is mostly restricted to legal documents. Fr: Marin; Ger: Nautiker; Seafahrer."

"MERCHANT MARINE: The ships and vessels belonging to a maritime nation and employed in commerce and trade. Also called merchant navy (G.B.), mercantile marine. Fr: Marine Marchande; Marine de Commerce; Ger: Handelsmarine."

"MERCHANT SEAMAN: A name given to a seaman on a private vessel as distinguished from seamen in the Navy or on public vessels."

"MERCHANT VESSEL: A privately owned vessel employed and managed by traders for commerce and transportation. Also called trading vessel, merchantman, commercial vessel...Fr: Batiment de Commerce; Navire Marchand; Ger: handelsschiff; Kauffahrteischiff."

"PUBLIC VESSEL: A vessel owned or chartered by a State or by the ruler of a State for carrying out public duties such as the transportation of troops, ammunition, stores, scientific expeditions. Men-of-war and naval auxiliaries are immediately identified with the personality of the State. Both on the high seas and in foreign ports, they are floating portions of the territory of their state. They may not, as neutrals, be visited, searched or detained by belligerents. Public vessels include dispatch vessels, school ships, naval colliers, revenue vessels, lighthouse tenders and generally all vessels employed in the service of the state for public purposes only. According to the U. S. Tariff Act of 1922, only such vessels which are not permitted by the law of the nations to which they belong to be employed in the transportation of passengers or merchandise in trade are considered as public vessels. Fr: Mavire Public; Ger: Staatsdienstschiff.
     Great Britain, Foreign Office, Miscellaneous Papers 2 and
     8, 1938, INTERNATIONAL CONVENTION FOR THE UNIFICATION OF
     CERTAIN RULES CONCERNING THE IMMUNITY OF STATE OWNED SHIPS;
     Matsunami, N., IMMUNITY OF STATE SHIPS, London, 1924; U. S.
     Naval War College, "The Classification of Public Vessels,"
     INTERNATIONAL LAW TOPICS, Washington, 1915."

[INTERNATIONAL MARITIME DICTIONARY, by Rene deKerchove, Second Edition, Van Nostrand Reinhold, 1961, New York, London.]

SHIPS OF WAR

"SHIP OF WAR":   British Naval regulations of 1912 contained this
definition: "The term 'ship of war' is to be understood as
including all ships designated as such in the accepted sense of the
term   and   also   auxiliary   vessels   of   all   descriptions."
[INTERNATIONAL LAW SITUATIONS, 1930, Naval War College, Washington
1931, Page 10.]

* * *

"ACQUIRING CHARACTER OF ENEMY WARSHIP" Merchant Vessels [and
aircraft] acquire enemy character and are liable to the same
treatment as enemy warships [and military aircraft] (see Paragraph
503a) when engaging in the following acts:
    1.   Taking a direct part in the hostilities on the side of an
         enemy.
    2.   Acting in any capacity as a naval or military auxiliary to
         an enemy's armed force."

"503a Enemy Warship [and military aircraft]
    1)   Destruction.   Enemy   warships   [and   military   aircraft]
         (including naval and military auxiliaries) may be attacked
         and destroyed..."

[LAW OF NAVAL WARFARE, NWIP 10-2, Department of Navy, Office of the
Chief of Naval Operations, September 1955 (¶501 and ¶503).]

* * *

The term "merchant vessel and aircraft" therefore includes state
owned vessels and aircraft engaged in carrying persons or goods for
commercial purposes. [Footnote 3 for Chapter 5 from LAW OF NAVAL
WARFARE, NWIP 10-2, Department of the Navy, Office of the Chief of
Naval Operations, September 1955.]

TERMS AS UNDERSTOOD UNDER UNITED STATES STATUTES AND DECISIONS:

"PUBLIC VESSEL" means a vessel that
   A)   Is owned, or demise chartered, and operated by the United
        States Government or a government of a foreign country; and

   B)   Is not engaged in commercial service."

[Title 46 §2101 General Definitions (24) USCA]

"MERCHANT SEAMEN": Merchant seamen in this title simply means
seamen on private vessels as distinguished from seamen in the Navy
or on public vessels, and seamen employed on private vessels of all
nations are 'merchant seamen' and literally included in this
phrase.   U.S. v. Sullivan, C.C.Or. 1890, 43 F. 602.   See also
Scharrenberg v. Dollar S. S. Company., Cal. 1917, 38 S Ct. 28, 245
U.S. 122, 62 L.Ed. 189." [See Title 46 §713 Note 15, USCA.]

LAW

COMMON LAW: "1. The sytem of laws originated and developed in England, based on court decisions, on the doctrines implicit in those decisions and on customs and usages, rather than on codified written law. 2. The part of a system of laws of any state or nation that is of a general and universal application."
[THE AMERICAN HERITAGE DICTIONARY OF THE ENGLISH LANGUAGE, 1969.]

INTERNATIONAL LAW: "The law which regulates the intercourse of nations. 1 Kent, Comm. 1, 4. The customary law which determines the rights and regulates the intercourse of independent states in peace and war."
[BLACKS LAW DICTIONARY, Revised Fourth Edition, West Publishing company, 1968.]

INTERNATIONAL MARITIME LAW: "The system of rules which civilized states acknowledge between them and which relates to the affairs and business of the sea, to ships, their crews and to marine conveyance of persons and property. Also called international law of the sea. International maritime law is divided into public and private international maritime law. The former consists of the rules adopted for the settlement of questions relating directly to sovereign states, the latter of those adopted for settling litigations between subjects belonging to different nations.
[Gainer, J. W., INTERNATIONAL LAW AND THE WORLD WAR, London 1920; Hall, W. E., TREATISE ON INTERNATIONAL LAW, London 1925; Oppenheim, L. F. L., INTERNATIONAL LAW, London 1935; Pierce Higgins and Columbos, THE INTERNATIONAL LAW OF THE SEA, London 1943.
[INTERNATIONAL MARITIME DICTIONARY, by Rene De Kerchove, Second Edition, Van Nostrand Reinhold, 1961, New York, London.]

STATUTE LAW: "A law established by legislative enactment.
[AMERICAN HERITAGE DICTIONARY OF THE ENGLISH LANGUAGE, 1969.]

CHARTER FORMS

BAREBOAT CHARTER: 1. "Same as demise charter." [INTERNATIONAL MARINE DICTIONARY.] 2. "Lease of a ship without equipment or crew." [NAVAL TERMS DICTIONARY, Fourth Edition, Noel and Beach, Naval Institute Press, Annapolis, 1978.] 3. "Charterers obtain the complete control of the vessel which they are operating as if she belonged to their own fleet. All costs and expense incident to the use and operation of the vessel are for charterer's account. Charterer will keep the vessel in good running order and condition and in substantially the same condition as when delivered by her owners. They will have her regularly overhauled and repaired as necessary." [CHARTERING AND SHIPPING TERMS, by J.Bes, Fourth Edition, Amsterdam, 1956.]

SUB-BAREBOAT CHARTER: "An agreement made by the charterer of a vessel to sublet in part or totally, the said vessel to other persons." [INTERNATIONAL MARINE DICTIONARY]
          As the term is applied to the situation in World War II with War Shipping Administration charters, it would refer to vessels bareboat chartered from owners by WSA and then subsequently sub-bareboated by WSA to another party. This was an arrangement commonly used prior to late 1943 by WSA when transferring vessels to Army control wherein the Army crewed and otherwise fully operated the vessel. Following 1943, the practice of sub-bareboat chartering was curtailed in favor of the practice of "allocating" WSA vessels to the carriage of military cargoes and personnel under "allocation;" WSA remained the vessel's operators.

DEMISE CHARTER: Another term for "bareboat charter." "A charter in which the bare ship is chartered without crew." [INTERNATIONAL MARINE DICTIONARY]

TIME CHARTER: "A form of charter party issued when the vessel is chartered for an agreed period of time. It places the vessel in the possession of the charterer. It may, however, provide that the owner shall man and provision the vessel. In ocean traffic, the usual practice is for the charterer to pay to the owner for the hire of the ship an agreed rate per deadweight ton per month and to furnish the fuel and pay all expenses at the ports except crew and provision expenses. [INTERNATIONAL MARINE DICTIONARY]

EXPLANATION OF CITATIONS WITHIN THE TEXT.

Because of the nature of this treatise, as an aid
to the reader who will utilize this publication within his
own research efforts, the following format has been
utilized for purposes of identifying the source of
quotations, etc.

The first time a publication is utilized, the
entire name of the publication, author, et al, are given
in single space following the appropriate text. In those
instances where a publication is cited again, only a "key
word or phrase" appears along with the volume, if
applicable, and the page number(s). Usually the key word
is the author's last name; or, in lieu of that, the title
of the quoted publication or paper.

Example:
Initial mention: See Page 5 Citation
    [POLICY OF THE UNITED STATES TOWARD MARITIME COMMERCE
    IN WAR, prepared by Carlton Savage, Volume I,
    1776-1914, the Department of State 1934, Government
    Printing Office, Washington, DC, Page 119.]

Subsequent mention: See Page 8 Citation
    [Savage, Volume I, Page 37.]

Reader is referred to the Bibliography Section
for complete listing of all cited documents as well as
additional works which were used as references.

PART I

COLONIAL ERA TO WORLD WAR II

COLONIAL ERA

The transformation of our merchant marine into an arm of our naval force during World War II came about through a long term development in both international practices and treaties as well as through the internal acts of many nations. Its beginnings, as a merchant marine and the things which contributed to its transformation had their start during the Colonial period.

* * * * * * * *

Those British colonies which later became the United States, had under localized registry a fleet of commercial vessels used in both the coastal and in the foreign trades. That fleet's primary purpose was that of peaceful commerce, although at times, such as during the French and Indian Wars, some of the vessels were used as sea raiders (privateers) operating under British license to seize the goods and ships of Britain's enemies. Vessels operating as privateers remained under the full commercial control of their owners and therefore retained, as private vessels, their identification as merchant ships. Their crews were not part of the British Naval establishment even though they were recognized under international practice as combatants and commonly treated as legitimate prisoners of war whenever captured.

With the advent of the American Revolution, a sizeable portion of the ownership of the merchant fleet then registered in the Colonies sided with the revolutionary movement. Most were kept in commercial coastal trade during the war. Some of them intermittently aided in logistical support to the Continental Army and to State Militia forces. In the first months of the Revolution (August 1775 to October 1776), a few merchant ships were militarized and used as public commerce raiders under the control and manning of the Continental Army. Following October 1776, the Continental Army, for the most part, ceased operating combatant ships--the one exception to this being the building of a small fleet assembled on Lake Champlain by Brigadier General Benedict Arnold. With this fleet, Arnold delayed, but could not halt, the British advance from Canada southward to the Hudson Valley.

In October of 1776, the Continental Congress authorized the purchase of two vessels to operate under the mandate of a "Naval Committee" thus marking the

official birth of the Continental Navy. From that point
onward, there was a clear distinction between merchant
ships, including privateers, and commissioned Naval
vessels.

The value of merchant shipping and privateers to
the winning of the war was immeasurable. This especially
applied to the privateers.

"No group of individuals did more for
establishing our country than the American Merchant Seamen
and Privateers. Their record speaks eloquently of their
devotion and sacrifices." [Memoirs of John Adams.]

THE PEACE

A proposition for immunity of private property at sea in time of war was first suggested by Benjamin Franklin in 1780. In 1783, it was presented by the American commissioners, then negotiating peace with Great Britain, for inclusion in the treaty plan. The Continental Congress did include the proposition in the formalized treaty of 1784. It was embodied also within the first treaty signed with Prussia. The proposition outlined on all three occasions was that in case of war between the parties, the ordinary commerce of belligerent nationals should not be molested and that privateers would not be commissioned to interrupt such commerce. The extent to which immunity should prevail against armed public ships was left in doubt. It does not appear from the language of the proposition, however, that the immunity of commerce in ordinary commodities extended to the special trade of supplying armed forces with implements of war.

[POLICY OF THE UNITED STATES TOWARD MARITIME COMMERCE IN WAR, prepared by Carlton Savage, Volume I, 1776-1914, the Department of State 1934, Government Printing Office, Washington, DC, Page 119.]

THE QUASI-WAR 1798-1801

During the Quasi-War with France, the status of the commercial merchant marine appears to have remained unchanged from that of its regular peacetime character. There were probably no American vessels devoted primarily to privateering although the Congressional Act of July 9, 1798 permitted American merchant ships to capture French armed vessels. Since most merchant ships were normally armed during this period, the result was a number of engagements between American and French merchantmen.

[OUR NAVAL WAR WITH FRANCE, by Gardner W. Allen, Houghton Mifflin Company, Boston and New York 1909.]

THE WAR OF 1812

When war broke out again with Britain, merchant ship owners responded energetically in a spirit of patriotism flavored with the lure of private profit. Privateering became big business, and owners armed and crewed their ships solely for the purpose of cruising the high seas on the lookout for prizes. In this, they were highly successful, providing more of a harassment to Britain than did our Navy. During this period, privateers sailed under the authorization of the Congress through Letters of Marque. The crews, as in the past, were treated as legal combatants and when captured, were handled as prisoners of war. In a legal sense, the ships retained their identification as vessels of commerce (merchantmen) since governmental control consisted only of their masters requiring a license to operate against the enemy's shipping. If a privateer was captured, its status was essentially the same as that of a man-of-war -- the ship becoming enemy property following adjudication.

In summarizing United States policy concerning the Government's instructions to privateers during the War

of 1812, Carlton Savage holds that none of those
instructions contained detailed mention of the
controversial questions concerning neutral commerce. They
merely provided that the commander was to "pay the
strictest regards to the rights of neutral powers and the
usages of civilized nations." The commanders of armed
ships were left to determine for themselves, from general
knowledge and published authorities, as to what were the
rights in question, subject of course to rulings of prize
courts and to the generally understood standards of
International Law. [Savage, Volume I, Page 37.]

MEXICAN WAR

1846-1848

The Mexican War marked the first wartime utilization of the Merchant Marine through the vehicle of government control. According to historian Erna Risch, the Army's Quartermaster Corps had upward of one hundred and three vessels of all classes under its direct control either through ownership or demise charter. Beyond the number under its complete control, the War Department time chartered merchant ships for specific operations. The highest volume of merchant shipping was used for the landings at Vera Cruz where one hundred sixty-three ships originated from Gulf of Mexico ports with another fifty-three originating from east coast ports.

[QUARTERMASTER SUPPORT OF THE ARMY, A HISTORY OF THE CORPS, 1775-1939, by Erna Risch, Quartermaster Historians Office, Office of the Quartermaster General, Washington, DC, 1962, Chapter VII.]

MID - CENTURY

President Pierce, in a message to Congress dated December 4, 1854, said that he felt that an international treaty might be in order to protect merchant shipping. He wrote:

> "If the leading European powers should concur in proposing, as a rule of International Law, to exempt private property upon the ocean from seizure by public armed vessels as well as by privateers, the United States would readily meet them upon that broad ground." [Savage, Volume I, Page 75.]

PRIVATEERING AND THE DECLARATION OF PARIS

In 1856 accredited representatives of all recognized maritime powers met to establish a basis of conduct in the future waging of sea warfare. Four major points were agreed on. Two pertained to the rights of neutrals and their goods; another covered law of blockade. The fourth point stated:

"Privateering is, and remains, abolished."

All nations present signed with the exception of the United States, Spain, Mexico, and Venezuela.

"The Declaration of Paris in Modern War," LAW QUARTERLY REVIEW, London, Vol 55, 1939, pp 237-49.]

Even though the treaty was not signed by the United States, the other major maritime nations had negated the future existence of privateering. In the eyes of the signers, international jurists would now have to deal with only two classes of ships -- warships and merchantmen. No gray areas of use seemed to be left to cloud the legal scene.

The fact that the United States and Spain did not sign seems now, in retrospect, to have been a rather moot issue as ten years prior, in 1846, the EL UNICO, holding a

Letter of Marque from the Mexican government (against which we were then at war) captured the American merchant ship CARMELITA and took her into Barcelona, Spain. The Spanish arrested the EL UNICO crew on charges of piracy and returned the American ship to her owners. The United States, for its part, had shortly before declared that privateers operating against American shipping would be treated as pirates, and a law to that effect had been enacted by Congress.

During the Civil War, the U. S. Congress authorized that Letters of Marque be issued by the President; however Lincoln never acted on that authorization. The Confederates, on the other hand appear to have encouraged privateering, as exemplified by Jefferson Davis's Proclamation of April 17, 1861, that was followed by Confederate Congressional authorization setting up the mechanism for granting Letters of Marque. In all, forty-nine Confederate vessels were licensed as privateers; however, only seventeen actually saw privateering service. At first, the Union embarked on policy of treating captured privateer crews as pirates, indicting three such crews on that charge; but under threat of retaliation against Union prisoners being held by the Confederacy, these crews were eventually treated as legitimate prisoners of war.

[THE DICTIONARY OF AMERICAN FIGHTING SHIPS, Volume II, Naval History Division, U. S. Navy, Washington, DC, Pages 584-85.]

[HISTORY OF THE CONFEDERATE STATES NAVY, By J. Thomas Scharf, reprinted by the Fairfax Press.]

CIVIL WAR

The use of merchant shipping by both the Union
and Confederate forces was extensive. The Union side,
through the dictates of favorable geography which gave it
control of sea access, made heavy use of shipping in
virtually all of its campaigns. This was not confined
only to coastal zones. The penetration of the south by
the Union's Armies of the West depended almost entirely on
the Mississippi River and its tributaries.

The overall magnitude of shipping utilized during
the War has been focused on by Erna Risch in his
QUARTERMASTER SUPPORT OF THE ARMY. Risch's studies tell
us that for ocean and coastwise service, the Union Army
purchased and built a total of 183 ocean steamers, 43
sailing vessels and 86 barges; while it chartered "or
otherwise hired" at one time or another, 753 ocean
steamers, 1080 sailing vessels, and 847 barges. On the
western rivers, the Union Army ended up owning 599 "boats"
91 of which were steamers and the rest barges and assorted
work boats. Another group consisting of 633 steamers and
139 other assorted craft were chartered, hired, or

temporarily commandeered for use during the period of the western campaigns.

> Note: My own review of Quartermaster reports indicates that the number of vessels mentioned by Risch as being chartered is somewhat misleading since, in a number of cases, the same vessel was chartered more than once.

On east coast inland waters such as the Chesapeake Bay and Virginia river systems, there were Union Army fleets in use for specific campaigns. For instance, in the northern Virginia campaign of 1862, approximately four hundred river craft were employed as troop carriers and supply vessels; most of these were chartered.

Generally speaking, both the Union and the Confederacy looked upon the other's shipping as legitimate targets of war with no apparent concern shown by either side as to whether the vessels were combatant type military supply boats, or even whether they were armed or unarmed. Armed and armored steamers utilized on the Mississippi as Army gun boats carried mixed civilian and military crews as a fairly regular thing. Crew composition seemed to be more a matter of availability. This appears to have been the first time in our history where civilians and military were intermingled in the manning of vessels of the Army or Navy. A generalized inquiry into the history of the Civil War based upon my

own reading of published and Archival file material, as
well as discussions with those expert in the field, has
disclosed nothing that would indicate policy questions
arising during 1861-65 over the utilization of these mixed
crews on warships.

THE DRAFT EXEMPT ACT OF 1896

On May 28, 1896, the Congress of the United States passed into law an Act entitled LICENSE TO OFFICERS OF VESSELS OF THE UNITED STATES; EXEMPTION FROM DRAFT; PAY AND PENSIONS [c255 §29 Stat. 188].

The primary purpose of this law was to establish standards for the renewal of merchant marine officer licenses and create procedures by which disciplinary actions could be taken against such licenses. The statute also established that licensed officers were to be exempt from

"...draft in time of war, except for the performance of duties such⌐ as are required by his licences; and while performing such duties in the service of the United States every master, mate, pilot, or engineer shall be entitled to the highest rate of wages paid in the merchant marine of the United States for similar services; and if killed or wounded while performing such duties under the United States, they, or their heirs, or their legal representatives, shall be entitled to all the privileges accorded to soldiers and sailors serving in the Army or Navy under the pension laws of the United States."

From an historian's viewpoint, the social aspects of the legislation is interesting in that from the standpoint of the granting of pensions, it ignores any mention of unlicensed personnel. Between 1880 and 1895, the American merchant marine had reached the most depressed point in its history. Few of the unlicensed men of that day possessed U.S. citizenship. Taken as a group, unlicensed seamen ranks contained a high proportion of drifters and other undesirables. Young Americans of that period rarely considered going to sea in an unlicensed capacity other than as apprenticed cadets. On the other hand, licensed officers were mainly U. S. citizens, and they were of a class generally educated beyond the level required for most occupations ashore. It is therefore understandable that in 1896 the licensed man was singled out for special benefits. It is surprising, though, that when this Act was continued, through recodification in 1914, 1936, and 1946, and again as late as 1983, that the social injustice of the pension aspect was never rectified. In fact, as I can ascertain from reading the Act's legislative history, no one appears to have observed that the wording contained such an injustice.

Aside from the discrimatory aspects of the legislation, the Act is significant in that it is one of the earliest pieces of Congressional thinking to indicate concern for a future need for a professional force of mariners which would be on hand in time of war to man ships in support of the naval or military effort.

SPANISH AMERICAN WAR

The war with Spain (1898) was preceeded by considerable saber rattling beginning in 1897 through the efforts of the Hearst newspapers. Despite this, the U. S. military did not actually start planning for hostilities until the sinking of the USS MAINE in February of 1898. This provided little time for preparation. An American invasion force was to leave in May for the Spanish-held Philippine Islands; a month later, seventeen thousand invasion troops would leave Tampa, Florida, bound for Santiago, Cuba. One problem brought on by the lack of pre-planning was a severe shortage of shipping equipped to handle troops and their equipment. This in turn caused an almost endless series of things going wrong; however, thanks to United States control of the sea routes and just plain good luck, nothing of really disastrous proportions occurred although it is probably correct to observe that logistically the Spanish American War did not run anywhere near as smoothly as that of the Civil War.

Fortunately for its participants, the war with Spain was short-lived. Peace negotiations started on the first of October of 1898, just four months following the start of hostilities.

Significant to the purpose of this paper are the lessons learned from that "splended little war." As a result of the obvious need for improvement, the Army's Quartermaster recommended the creation of this country's first permanent seagoing supply force, organized as part of the military establishment. Named the Army Transport Service (ATS), it was formalized on November 16, 1898, as part of the Quartermaster Corps, to be administered by officers of the Corps. The masters, officers, and crews of the vessels were civilian employees.

> Note: The ATS would continue operations under various organizational alteration until disbanded in the 1950s when the Navy took over the operation. At that time, the command came to be known as the Military Sea Transport Service. Still operational under the Navy, this organization was again renamed and is today called the Military Sealift Command.

As envisioned by its creators in 1898, the Army's ATS was to be run in peacetime along the organizational lines utilized by civilian steamship companies. This was a policy long followed since it was successful both in terms of efficiency as well as in cost effectiveness. It was not until 1938 that the role of the Army Transport Service began changing in part to one of tactical employment whe

certain of its transports were used during amphibious
exercises working in conjunction with the Navy off the
Carolina coast and off Puerto Rico.

THE DECLARATION OF LONDON -1909

The "Declaration of London" was signed by all the
major powers including Germany, the United States,
Austria, Hungary, Spain, France, Great Britain, Italy,
Japan, the Netherlands, and Russia.

Article 45 of the Declaration states,

"A neutral vessel will be condemned and will in a general
way receive the same treatment as a neutral vessel liable
to condemnation for carriage of contraband

"1)   if she is on a voyage, especially undertaken
with a view to the transport of individual passengers who
are embodied in the armed forces of the enemy, or with the
view to the transmission of intelligence in the interest
of the enemy.

"2)   if, to the knowledge of either the owner,
the charterer, or the master, she is transporting a
military detachment of the enemy or one or more persons
who, in the course of the voyage, directly assist the
operations of the enemy."

Article 46 of the Declaration states:

"A neutral vessel will be condemned and in a
general way receive the same treatment as would be
applicable to her if she were an enemy merchant vessel:

"1)   If she takes a direct part in the
hostilities.

"2)   If she is under the orders or control of an
agent placed on board by the enemy government.

"3)   If she is in the exclusive employment of the
enemy government.

"4)   If she is inclusively engaged at the time,
either in the transport of enemy troops or in the
transmission of intelligence in the interest of the enemy."

[POLICY OF THE UNITED STATES TOWARD MARITIME COMMERCE IN
WAR, prepared by Carlton Savage, Volume II, 1914-1918, the
Department of State 1936, Government Printing Office,
Washington, DC]

Although these Articles applied to the law of
blockade -- and specifically to neutral ships -- their
language is useful in determining the beginnings of a
categorization in thinking which would be applied to
merchant ships in time of war.

* * * * * *

The World War I experience has provided us with
the foundations of what is recognized today under
International Law.   To an historian, or to one with any
knowledge of the law, this "borrowing from the experience
of the past" should come as no surprise, since history
holds the seeds for all contemporary understanding.   To
help us to perceive what was to develop in the case of
shipping, it helps to know the meaning of certain relevant
terms which had become accepted prior to 1917, both
internationally and within the laws of the United States.

PUBLIC VESSELS - U. S. Law

Prior to the 1870s, there were few federal statutes effecting United States merchant shipping and merchant marine personnel. These dealt mainly with manning and safety and were known as the Inspection and Navigation Laws. Questions had arisen as to whether these regulatory statutes pertained also to vessels under public ownership. The exact meaning of the term "public vessel" was then in some doubt. The first definitive opinion was given by the Attorney General of the United States during 1870:

> "Public vessels, within the meaning of the inspection and navigation laws, are vessels owned by the United States and used by them for public purposes."

Legislation passed during 1871 excluded "Public Vessels" from regulatory authority imposed by the Inspection and Steam Vessel Act of February 28, 1871, [c.100, §41, 165 Stat 453]. The Steamboat Inspection Act of 1879 again excluded "public vessels" as earlier defined by the Attorney General's opinion rendered in 1870.

> Note: The meaning of "Public Vessel" and its usage under the U. S. Marine Inspection Laws remains the same today. The application of the term was broadened somewhat by case history dealing with the Public Vessel Liability Act of 1925 as discussed later in this volume. The Department of State and the Department of Navy policy current in 1986 claims public vessel sovereign immunity in practice only if applied to vessels under full governmental control;

nevertheless, the juridical argument is made by the Department of State that this could be extended to cover all vessels engaged in military employment. (Appendix D reproduces the complete government policy statement.)

CLASS OF GOODS -- International Practice

Prior to World War I, the relationship of a vessel's cargo to the vessel was considered a deciding element in judging a merchant vessel's role. This was especially pertinent toward determining a merchant vessel's fate when it was intercepted by a blockading warship. Chief Justice Salmon P. Chase of the U. S. Supreme Court, writing toward the end of the Civil War expressed what he believed was the general concensus at that time:

"Of these [cargo] classes the first consists of articles manufactured and primarily and ordinarily used for military purposes in time of war; the second, of articles which may be and are used for purposes of war or peace according to circumstances; and the third of articles exclusively used for peaceful purposes. Merchandise of the first class, destined to a belligerent country...is always contraband; merchandise of the second class is contraband only when actually destined to the military or naval use of a belligerent; while merchandise of the third class is not contraband at all, though liable to seizure and condemnation for violation of blockade."

Vice Admiral Hyman G. Rickover, writing in September 1935 in the U. S. Naval Institute PROCEEDINGS, when still a lieutenant, made a major point that the type of cargo a ship carried was no longer significant in light

of the conditions of modern submarine warfare. He was, of
course, speaking of the situation which had developed
during the first World War. In his article, Rickover
quoted Sir Edward Grey of the British Foreign Ministry.
In a communication to the American government made on
February 10, 1915, Grey had claimed that no country in
modern times had maintained more stoutly than Great
Britain the principle that a belligerent should abstain
from interference with the shipment of foodstuffs intended
for the civil population of the enemy; however, Grey
doubted whether the principle was still applicable past
1915, in view of the fact that the German government had
by then taken over control of the entire German food
supply. Because of that nationalization, Great Britain
had abolished any distinction it had earlier placed
between absolute and conditional contraband. On April 13,
1916, it announced through its Foreign Office:

> "His Majesty's Government considers that for
> practical purposes, the distinction between absolute and
> conditional contraband has ceased to have any value."

> Note: Taking the matter forward to World War II,
> one can see very little practical
> distinction--when measured on a military value
> scale--between a tanker loaded with refined
> petroleum transiting from Texas up the U. S. east
> coast to fuel a fully mobilized civilian economy
> geared for war and a sister ship carrying
> petroleum transatlantic to North Africa to fuel
> the vehicles of an armoured division directly

engaged with the enemy. The Germans seemed to be of similar opinion as attested to by their heavy assaults against U. S. east coast tanker shipments during 1942-43. Global sea war, as viewed in the light of the naval experience of both World Wars, was largely an attempt to destroy the enemy's means of overall logistical support. In the case of the Battle of the Atlantic (period 1942-43), the Germans did not strategically discriminate even between loaded or unloaded ships, their major purpose being to win the tonnage war of attrition--in other words, to sink Allied ships faster than they could be built.

It can safely be said that following 1915 and throughout the entirety of World Wars I and II, no distinction was made by any of the antagonists as to "class of goods," or as to whether a ship was loaded or in ballast, when determining its warlike status.

WORLD WAR I

With the onset of the First World War, the United
States government took steps to rebuild its merchant
marine from what, over the years, had degenerated to
becoming merely a fleet of coastal traders.   With the
vacuum created in world commerce by the evolvement of the
European powers in war, the opportunity could be seen a
early as 1914 that a modern oceangoing fleet o
merchantmen sailing under the American flag could become
the predominant factor in world trade.   The biggest
stumbling block to such a program was the unavailability
of private capital to make it all work.   To surmount this
the federal government undertook plans for a massive ship
building program.   Ships were constructed by Government
and then chartered out to private operators (and even to
its own governmental sub agencies).   The legal apparatus
for this was announced within the Preamble to the Shipping
Act of 1916:

> "To establish a United States Shipping Board fo
> the purpose of encouraging, developing, and creating
> naval auxiliary and naval reserve and a merchant marine t
> meet the requirements of the commerce of the United State
> with its Territories and possessions and with foreig
> countries;..."

The Shipping Act, as passed by Congress on 7 September 1916, contained a provisional clause for the operation of vessels purchased, chartered, or leased from the United States Shipping Board by private operators:

"Such vessels, while employed solely as merchant vessels, shall be subject to all laws, regulations and liabilities governing merchant vessels, whether the United States be interested therein as owner, in whole or in part, or hold any mortgage, lien, or other interest therein."

Professor Jeffrey Safford discusses the political strategy used in passing the Act:

"Wilson sidestepped private capital's resistance to a government shipping program by adroitly marketing the merchant fleet as an auxiliary force for the Navy. 'It was the expedient thing to do,' McAddoo [President Wilson's Secretary of the Treasury] later remarked, upon the Administration's strategy: 'people as a rule are far more interested in fighting, and in preparation for fighting, then they are in any constructive commercial or industrial effort.'"

"America's Maritime Legacy: A History of the U. S. Merchant Marine and Shipping Industry Since Colonial Times," by Professor Jeffrey J. Safford, A Westview Special Study, Westview Press, 1979] 1

In continuing his discussion over the intentions of the Act of 1916, the draftors of which had composed the Act long before the American involvement in the war and at a time when continued neutrality was still a hope, Safford theorized:

"Although its designers did not conceive of it as a means by which to provide transportation of soldiers and equipment to the French front, the Act was passed for the

purpose of encouraging developing and creating a nava
auxiliary and naval reserves'--a clear understanding o
new realitites."

The Act of 1916 is helpful in developing

perspective for what was to follow, as this was,

believe, the first time, that a distinction was made unde

U. S. law between the terms, "Naval Auxiliary" and "Nava

Reserve," as those terms were used in describing the us

of ships. When applied specifically to merchant vessels

the term "auxiliary" as defined within the INTERNATIONA

MARITIME DICTIONARY:

"AUXILIARY VESSEL: A term applied generally to al
merchant ships and pleasure craft whether belligerent o
neutral used for the transportation of enlisted men
munitions of war, fuel, provisions, water, or any othe
kind of naval supplies; also those which are designed a
repair ships or charged with the carrying of dispatches o
the transmission of information, specifically if sai
vessels are obliged to carry out the sailing orders give
them directly or indirectly by a belligerent fleet.
merchantman which transfers, by its own act, to wa
vessels, the fuel which it has aboard either as cargo o
bunkers is considered an auxiliary vessel to the war flee
to which delivery has been made..."2

The term "Naval Reserve" as it appeared in th

Act of 1916, referred, in that case, to passenger an

cargo bottoms available for direct naval requisitioning

once requisitioned, they would be handled as commissione

vessels operating in direct support of the fleet, ie.

fleet auxiliaries.

The Shipping Act of 1916 legislatively single

ut the merchant marine as having a wartime role in the nation's defense posture. No other industrial or commercial segment of the U. S. economy had, either by subsidy or policy, been so predesignated for nationalized control. (Upon U. S. entry into the war, the railroads were nationalized but that was a step which had not been legislatively predetermined.)

When the U. S. finally entered the First World War as a belligerent, the potential war powers which had been incorporated within the wording of the Shipping Act were put in force through the Act of Congress of June 17, 1917, authorizing the President of the United States:

> "To purchase, requisition, or take over the title to, or the possession of, for use or operation by the United States, any ship now constructed or in process of construction or hereafter constructed, or any part thereof, or charter of such ship."

The circumstantial basis for purchase or requisition was given within the Prelude to the 1917 Act as being for the purpose of "military exigency" and for purposes essential to the prosecution of the war." That Act, although conceptually concerned with procurement of ships for the Army and Navy, also established means by which Government agencies other than the Army and Navy could also take over shipping. The requisitioning by a standard form of Presidential Executive Order was the legal mechanism by which transfer to government service took place. The ship was then turned over to either the Army or Navy or to a civilian agency known as the United States Shipping Board.

The terms of the requisition authority expressly stipulated that such ships

"shall not have the status of a public ship and shall be subject to all laws and regulations governing merchant vessels. When, however, the requisitioned vessel is engaged in the service of the War or Navy Departments, the vessel shall have the status of a public ship and the masters, officers, and crew should become the immediate employees and agents of the United States with all the rights and duties of such, the vessel passing completely into the possession of the masters, officers, and crew absolutely under the control of the United States."

[INTERNATIONAL LAW SITUATIONS, 1930, Page 49]

The requisition charter stipulated that the "master" shall be the agent of the owner in all matters respecting the management, handling, and navigation of the vessel, except when the vessel becomes a "public ship."

Professor J. R. Smith in his THE INFLUENCE OF SHIPPING described this transfer of private enterprise to governmental control: "The Official mind replaces supply and demand." No longer were trade and commerce the purposes for our oceangoing merchant marine; it had now become, as it was described by George Grafton Wilson writing in 1931, "a war purpose and the ships were run for war ends."

Complete control does not, however, appear to have been inclusive of the entirety of the United States merchant marine (1917-18) since coastal shipping continued pretty much along the lines of the pre-war commercially oriented operation. A similar scenario applied for most of the Pacific trade routes.

Under the war powers granted the Shipping Board, requisition authority over private shipping in its practice extended to all power driven steel cargo vessels of over 2,500 deadweight tons as well as to all passenger vessels over 2,500 gross tons which were used for ocean service. At its option, the Shipping Board, when taking over a ship, could enter into either a "requisition time charter" or a "requisition bareboat charter."

While addressing the utilization of those ships which were under the ownership of the U. S. Shipping Board, Professor Jeffrey Safford states that two thirds of them were used on the European war run; the remaining third carried on global trade, most of which contributed to the support of industrial production eventually destined for the American Expeditionary Force (AEF) and Allied armies in Europe.

Part of the U. S. merchant fleet that went under direct government control during 1917-18 was operated by the Shipping Board which manned its ships from the maritime work force. The Army operated its ships with Civil Service crews under the employ of the Army Transport Service. The Navy's crewing programs varied with some civilian crews and some military. Other ships which were assigned to the Navy were attached directly to the fleet, becoming fleet auxiliaries; all of those had Naval crews.

Edward N. Hurley who was the wartime chairman of the U. S. Shipping Board, claimed that at the close of the war, the United States had seven million deadweight tons in its deep sea fleet of merchant class ships. Of that, he claimed four and a half million tons were manned by civilian crews with the rest by the Navy.

[THE BRIDGE TO FRANCE, by Edward N. Hurley, J. B. Lippincott Company, Philadelphia, 1927.]

> Note: Hurley fails to separate out those War Department ships which were a part of the overall sealift upon which Hurley seems to have based his numbers.

Some ships which were owned by or under charter to the Shipping Board were transferred to the War Department or to the Navy. In such cases, they were transferred by the Shipping Board on a bareboat or sub-bareboat (demise) basis, with manning, victualing, and all costs of operating accruing to the charterer--such vessels thereafter being officially designated as Army or Navy transports for the period of that charter. A similar bareboat arrangement applied in other cases to ships in direct Government service which were operated for the Government by agents responsible to the Shipping Board. The Agent received a commission or a stipulated fee for management services. Some of the requisitioned ships which were operated by agents were placed on time charters and were put into commercial trade by the agent until they were needed for the specific carriage of military cargo at which time the Shipping Board, exercising its ongoing authority, would reassign the ship, still under time charter, to that military purpose. This last arrangement turned out to be a workable system which allowed normal trade to continue whenever possible but with the priority always being on military requirements. The practicality of such programs were such that similar arrangements, with some refinement, were followed during World War II.

The increasing burden of fighting an overseas war soon brought the Army to the conclusion that the running of a fleet of ocean transports and cargo ships in transatlantic service was taxing its already overstretched capabilities. With Presidential concurrence, the Navy agreed to take over those Army ships in that service as soon as trained Naval crews were ready. All new transports coming from the shipyards were to be Navy operated and manned. Prior to the Navy takeover, joint planning by Army, Navy, and the Shipping Board took place in June of 1918. The following month, the Shipping Board wrote Josephus Daniels, Secretary of the Navy, laying out for his final consideration a prediscussed plan. Under that arrangement, the Navy was to take over manning of certain ships which were either at the time owned by the Shipping Board or which were in the planning stage for requisition by that agency. The plan called for:

"I. All troop ships and hospital ships are to be manned by the Navy.

"II. Armed transports and vessels engaged exclusively in the service of the War and/or Navy Departments are to be manned as directed by the interested department, which we understand will, in a great majority of cases, require that they be manned by Naval personnel.

"III. Commercial vessels engaged exclusively in the trade to ports within the war zone are to be manned by Naval personnel.

"IV. Commercial vessels engaged occasionally in trade as above, but which are likely to be sent to other ports in strictly commercial trade, are to be manned as far as possible, by merchant seamen.

"V. Commercial vessels engaged exclusively in safe trade, such as for instance, to West Indies, South America, Orient, Australia, and coastwise to be manned by merchant seamen."

A week after the plan's drafting, the Army requested of the Navy that in the next ninety days the Navy should take over, man, and operate:

"Transports manned by Army - 29
Transports manned by Shipping Board - 33
Transports manned by Owners - 23
Transports manned by Army abroad - 19
Transports manned by Shipping Board abroad - 20
Transports manned by Shipping Board on lakes - 30"

The Army, in its attempt to quickly divest itself of its responsibilities in operating or supervising the operations of troop transports, asked the Navy to begin by giving priority to the takeover of the Army's own transports. After the transfer of all troop transports, both Army and civilian run, a takeover was scheduled for Army cargo ships and tankers, but the war ended before that last plan was actually implemented. During 1917-18, the support of Army garrisons in the non-war zones, such as the western Pacific, remained, as it had been in pre-war days--the complete responsibility of the ATS.

[HISTORY OF THE NAVAL OVERSEAS TRANSPORTATION SERVICE IN WORLD WAR I, by Lewis P. Clephane and Naval History Division, Naval History Division, Washington, 1969, Pages 69-71.]

[MIXED CLAIMS COMMISSION (U. S. And Germany) ADMINISTRATIVE DECISIONS AND OPINIONS OF A GENERAL NATURE, to June 30, 1925, Library of Department of Justice, Washington, DC.]

DEALING WITH THE ARMING OF EUROPEAN MERCHANT SHIPS

WORLD WAR I

On 19 September 1914, the United States Department of State (the U. S. was neutral at that time) transmitted a Memorandum to foreign governments regarding its position on the presence of armament aboard foreign merchant vessels entering U. S. ports. The Memorandum addressed the sea war, as it was then being waged by surface vessels. When considering the intent as seen from the viewpoint of that day, it should be remembered that at that early point in the war, submarine warfare had not yet reached a point of dominance and therefore would not have been a prominant factor behind the composition of the State Department's 1914 thinking.

"A.   A merchant vessel of belligerent nationality may carry an armament and ammunition for the sole purpose of defense without acquiring the character of a ship of war.

"B.   The presence of an armament and ammunition on board a merchant vessel creates a presumption that the armament is for offensive purposes, but the owners or agents may overcome the presumption by evidence showing that the vessel carries armament solely for defense.

"C.   Evidence necessary to establish the fact that the armament is solely for defense and will not be used offensively, whether the armament be mounted or stowed below, must be presented in each case independently at an

official investigation. The result of the investigation
must show conclusively that the armament is not intended
for and will not be used in, offensive operations.
Indications that the armament will not be used offensively
are:

"1. that the caliber of the guns carried does not
     exceed six inches.

"2. that the guns and small arms carried are few in
     number.

"3. that no guns are mounted on the forward part of
     the vessel.

"4. that the quantity of ammunition carried is small.

"5. that the vessel is manned by its usual crew, and
     the officers are the same as those on board
     before war was declared.

"6. that the vessel intends to and actually does
     clear for a port lying on its usual trade route,
     or a port indicating its purpose to continue in
     the same trade in which it was engaged before war
     was declared.

"7. that the vessel takes on board fuel and supplies
     sufficient only to carry it to its port of
     destination, or the same quantity substantially
     which it has been accustomed to take for a voyage
     before war was declared.

"8. that the cargo of the vessel consists of articles
     of commerce unsuited for the use of a ship of war
     in operations against an enemy.

"9. that the vessel carries passengers who are as a
     whole unfitted to enter the military or naval
     service of the belligerent whose flag the vessel
     flies or of any of its allies, and particularly
     if the passenger list includes women and children.

"10. that the speed of the ship is slow."

[Department of State file 763.72111/226a; 1914 for Rel
Supp. 611-612]

This 1914 declaration of policy leaves the impression that its primary purpose was to differentiate a potential commerce raider from an ordinary merchantman armed for its own defense. It does, though, provide us with an early attempt by the Department of State to come to grips with the meaning of "offensively armed" as it would differ from the term "defensively armed,." a concern then gaining prominence within international diplomatic circles.

In a follow-up 1914 memorandum addressed to the Secretary of the Navy from the Department of State, the following question was put forth and then answered by State for the Navy's edification:

"Are the sailors of (merchant) ships armed for their own defense also belligerents in maritime war?"

"That depends on the status of those ships. If they are warships or ships assimilated to warships, their personnel should necessarily be considered as belligerents. But in general...defensively armed ships do not lose their former character; so their crews cannot have belligerent character any more than the ships themselves."

The concept of the sea war was in the process of great change, particularly because of the new type of warfare -- submarine against merchant ship. To help in countering this developing nemisis, the British Admiralty was, quite early, given full operational authority over the British merchant marine. This resulted in Admiralty guidelines issued in the form of orders to British ship masters covering, among other things, the arming of merchantmen and their general conduct in face of the enemy. These British orders were, on a number of counts, in marked conflict to the United States position taken in September 1914 regarding the guidelines for separating out defensively armed ships from those with offensive intentions.

The United States Secretary of State Robert Lansing therefore found it necessary to propose a restatement of principle regarding armed merchantmen. Within that statement, Lansing tried to put into focus the matter of armaments carried on those merchant ships which might become engaged in armed contest with submarines.

January 18, 1916:
"Even a merchant ship carrying a small caliber gun would be able to use it effectively for offense against a submarine. Moreover, pirates and sea rovers have been swept from the main trade channels of the seas and privateering has been abolished. Consequently, the placing of guns on merchantmen at the present day of submarine warfare can be explained only on the grounds of a purpose to render merchantmen superior in force to submarines and to prevent warning and visit and search by them. Any armament, therefore, on a merchant vessel would seem to have the character of an offensive armament."

Secretary Lansing's argument was not accepted by the British. It would later develop that other factors had to be considered:

Who controlled the ship?

Under what restrictions, if any, was the armament to be used?

Only the answers to those questions would determine if the armaments were "defensive" or "offensive." The case of the WOODFIELD, would not provide the answers, but it would help to bring some clarity into the argument.

On November 3, 1915, the WOODFIELD, a British merchant ship, was captured by a German submarine. Heavy fire directed against her by the attacker prevented the WOODFIELD's master from destroying his secret papers; these consequently came into the possession of the Germans. Among these papers were Admiralty instructions dated April 15, 1915, specifying actions that were to be taken against enemy submarines. Paragraphs 3 and 6 are reproduced:

"3. If a submarine is obviously pursuing a ship by day, and it is evident to the master that she has hostile intentions, the ship pursued should open fire in self defense, notwithstanding the submarine may not have committed a definite hostile act, such as firing a gun or torpedo."

"6. In view of the very great difficulty of distinguishing between friendly and hostile submarines at long range (one British submarine has already been fired at by a merchant vessel which erroneously supposed herself to be pursued by the submarine) it is strongly recommended that course (b) should be adopted by all defensively armed ships."

The quoted "course (b)" had said, "To retain fire

until the submarine has closed to a range, say 800 yards, at which fire is likely to be effective."
[INTERNATIONAL LAW SITUATIONS, 1930, Page 24]

Obviously, Paragraph 3 placed British merchant ships outside the realm of "fire only when fired upon."

Mallison, in INTERNATIONAL LAW STUDIES 1966, (Page 110) comments on the British orders captured with the WOODFIELD:

"It is interesting to apply this instruction to the situation where a submarine attempts to exercise the right of visit and search. [A right then given naval craft under established law.] The merchant ship master may reasonably believe that the submarine has 'hostile intentions,' so he may open fire first. In fact, almost any approach by a submarine could be regarded as pursuit of the merchant ship under the instruction."

Mallison footnotes this statement by adding a further comment which probably was made tongue -in- cheek:

"Shortly after the start of the First World War, [1914] the British had given the United States Government: the fullest assurance that British merchant vessels will never be used for purpose of attack, that they are merely peaceful traders armed only for defense, that they will never fire until first fired upon, and that they will never under any circumstances attack any vessel."

$$\# \quad \# \quad \# \quad \# \quad \# \quad \#$$

Author's Note: Professor William T. Mallison, occupied the Charles H. Stockton Chair of International Law at the Naval War College for the 1960-61 academic year. He is recognized by authorities as the person who in post World War II years authored the most comprehensive of all works on submarine warfare, including its relationship to merchant shipping. That work is entitled INTERNATIONAL LAW STUDIES, Naval War College, 1966, by W. T. Mallison, Jr., NAVPERS 15031, Volume LVIII. For legally minded students of World War II, Mallison's study is especially significant in that it was the first Naval War College study on the subject which included the utilization of previously classified Navy documents dealing with the U. S. Navy's attitudes relevant to our waging of the Pacific War against Japan's merchant fleet.

The orders of the British Admiralty had now
created a situation where merchant crews were to go beyond
the posture of defense to one of belligerent action. Out
of this grew yet another conundrum. Once having stepped
over the line, then at what point did the merchant crew
itself change character? Put another way, at what point,
if at all, did a merchant crew become part of a combatant
naval force? Or were their belligerent actions illegal in
light of International Law?

On June 23, 1916, German torpedo boats captured
the unarmed British merchantman BRUSSELS under the command
of Captain Charles A. Fryatt. Some months earlier in
1915, Fryatt had attempted to ram the German U-33. The
Germans claimed by attempting to ram, Fryatt had committed
an illegal act. After his capture in 1916, Fryatt was
taken to Germany where he was court martialed. The
specific premise was that by attempting to ram, he had
committed an unlawful act as a "franc- tireur," the charge
being "that while he was not a lawful member of a
combatant force, he had committed a combatant's act
against Germany." He was convicted and executed before a
firing squad.

Although unique in the experience of either of
the World Wars, the Fryatt case is highly important in

that it brings into focus the clear point of fact that if, in war, a person performs a hostile act in an attempt to wound or destroy his enemy, he is either one of two things:

(or)
> a legal combatant and therefore, in effect, a member of his nation's armed force--
>
> an illegal combatant and therefore subject to the same dire penalties afforded such persons as irregular partisans or disguised saboteurs.

He cannot be two things at any one time nor can he throw aside or assume at will a different character. To be a "legal combatant," he must have been ordered by his government to take part in hostilities against the enemy.

The Germans took the position that a merchantman was either assimilated to the naval force or remained innocent. On February 28, 1916, the German Foreign Office drafted a memorandum which it sent to the British Foreign Office:

> "The German Government has no doubt that a merchantman assumes a warlike character by armament with guns, regardless of whether the guns are intended to serve for defense or attack. It considers any warlike activity of an enemy merchantman contrary to international law, although it accords consideration to the opposite view by treating the crew of such a vessel not as pirates but as belligerents." [Under the general practice then in effect, legal belligerents (combatants) were treated as Prisoners of War.]

The U-33's commander testified:

> On approaching the BRUSSELS, he was exercising

humane procedures in trying to determine the merchant man's belligerent status through observation of her armament -- or lack of same -- before opening fire. The German alleged that it was during this investigatory approach that Fryatt tried to ram him. The German court's opinion was that Fryatt's ship did not have the authority to act as a combatant. Consequently, by trying to attack the submarine by ramming, Fryatt was acting as an illegal combatant.

An opposing viewpoint, which has since generally been taken by most students of the case, is that the lack of armament aboard the BRUSSELS had nothing to do with that ship's character as a belligerent combatant, since Admiralty instructions had all inclusively enfolded all British ships under the orders to initiate action toward the enemy.

To be sure, the Germans were well aware of those British orders at the time they took Fryatt as prisoner. What the critics of Fryatt's execution apparently do not realize is that Fryatt attempted to ram the U-33 on March 28, 1915, almost three weeks before the Admiralty instructions had been issued. In retrospect, it seems clear that the German charge was technically justified. By taking aggressive action without the instructions of his Government, Captain Fryatt had placed himself into the category of an illegal combatant.

1916

On January 17, 1916, U. S. Secretary of State Lansing, writing to President Wilson, said that there were reasonable arguments on both sides of the armament question. These led Lansing to the conclusion that the differences between the sides (Britain and Germany) had become "utterly irreconcilable." Lansing said he could see no common ground for making compromise. Wilson, writing back to Lansing on January 31, said that he felt that the British were going well beyond the spirit of the principle which he thought had previously settled the question with regard to the method in which armaments aboard merchant ships were to be used. Wilson felt the instructions issued to British ship masters on April 15, 1915, as to how they were to use their guns had exceeded that which could legitimately be called defense. The question became

'more, whether their guns had been used only for defense than whether they exceed in caliber what would reasonably constitute armament for defense and whether their being mounted in the bow is a presumption that they are to be used for offense."

Lansing, when stating his conclusions, wrote that he

believed in the principle that privately owned merchant
ships of enemy registry were entitled to defend
themselves. Accordingly, their treatment as being public
ships, just because they carried an armament adequate to
protect them from destruction, "can find no warrant in the
rules of naval warfare or in justice." Thus Lansing was
endorsing the established practice developed over the
years that arming of merchant vessels for defense was
legal and that such ships remained peaceable in character
as long as their intent was clearly defensive, meaning
that they did not operate under orders to fire on sight or
that they were not in some form incorporated within a
naval force. [Savage, Volume II, Page 80.]

Putting these principles of belief into the form
of United States policy, Lansing issued in March a
communique addressed to the German Foreign Ministry. Part
of the language in it would again be used in a Department
of State "white paper" to be released later that spring.

"A presumption based solely on the presence of an
armament on a merchant vessel is not a sufficient reason
for a belligerent to declare it to be a warship and
proceed to attack it without regard to the right of the
persons on board. Conclusive evidence of a purpose to use
the armament for aggression is essential...[A] belligerent
warship can on the high seas test by actual experience the
purpose of an armament on an enemy merchant vessel, and so
determine by direct evidence the status of the vessel."
[Foreign Rel U. S. suppl 245 246, 1916 (1929)]

The Secretary exhibited a naivete as to the realities of the sea war then being fought between Germany and Britain. Essentially, Lansing was saying to the belligerent powers that a submarine must first dangerously expose itself to the possibility of enemy initiated fire before the submarine would itself be justified in opening fire. No sane naval commander would have placed his submarine into such jeopardy. Lansing should have recognized this. In retrospect, what makes Lansing's memorandum seem especially unrealistic is that the world at large, including, I would presume, Secretary Lansing, knew that as early as November of 1914, the Royal Navy had commissioned and sent to sea its first "Q-Ship." With that event, an antagonist could no longer know whether he was approaching an ordinary merchantman or a disguised man-of-war.

Q SHIPS

"Q-Ship" was a synonym for a decoy ship which plied the seas disguised as a harmless merchantman. By operating under disguise, the Q-ship could lure submarines close aboard. Once the duped submarine had drawn sufficiently close, the Q-ship's false sides, and sometimes even a simulated deck house would fall away, exposing a gun battery. The vulnerable submarine would then be exposed to the full firepower of the more heavily armed Q-ship. The first British Q-ship, the VICTORIA failed to attract any victims, but the second one out was luckier. Named the SS PRINCE CHARLES, she was crewed by her original merchant officers and men but under the command of a Royal Navy lieutenant. A Navy gun crew manned the batteries. On July 24, 1915, the PRINCE CHARLES successfully lured in, fired upon, and sunk the U-36. This success resulted in the outfitting of a number of other Q-ships.

According to Q-SHIPS AND THEIR STORY by Kebel Chatterton: During World War I, eleven U-boat sinkings were made by disguised Q-ships.

Besides the kills, the Q-ships damaged at least eight more U-boats. The year 1916 marked the apex of Q-ship success as beyond that point, the submarine crews had learned the hard lesson that a merchant ship was all too often not what it seemed to be. The Royal Navy's use of Q-ships no doubt indirectly resulted in the deaths of many merchant seamen since U-boat commanders now had no alternative but to consider all merchantmen as potentially dangerous. U-boatmen began shooting first in almost all instances. In August of 1917, the British lost three Q-ships to suspicious U-boats. This led to the immediate abandonment of the decoy ships as an effective antisubmarine weapon.

In 1917, the United States Navy tried the Q-ship concept at least once but without success. The American experiment, the Q-ship SANTEE, was torpedoed on her first voyage and without getting the sub that got her.
[THE BATTLE OF THE ATLANTIC, U. S. NAVAL OPERATIONS IN WW II, Volume I, by Samuel Eliot Morison, Atlantic Little Brown, 1970; Footnote 13, p. 382.]

Thanks in part to the British use of Q-ships, the argument over what was a harmless merchantmen and what was not, and whether or not merchant seamen were combatants, legal or otherwise, had completely gone by the board. The British and the Germans by 1917 had turned the seas into a bloody cauldron where no distinctions were being made and where 'no quarter' was generally the rule.

> Note: During World War II, both the British and
> the United States navies again tried the Q-Ship
> approach. Neither Navy had any success, and the
> experiments were soon dropped. The Germans had
> remembered the lessons learned during 1916.

THE UNITED STATES MEMORANDUM OF MARCH 25, 1916

On March 25, 1916, the U. S. Secretary of State, Robert Lansing, signed a comprehensive Memorandum regarding sea warfare   On April 27, 1916, it was issued in summarized form within a circular telegram sent to certain European countries (Britain and Germany included) and to Japan. [State Department (File No. 763.72/2636a)] The memorandum prelude proclaimed:

"The status of an armed merchant vessel of a belligerent is to be considered from two points of view: First, from that of a neutral when the vessel enters its port; and second, from that of an enemy when the vessel is on the high seas."

The full content of this 1916 Memorandum would establish the basis for United States policy as applicable to World War I.   It would also effect policy and decisions in World War II and is still pertinent to the present day, being, to a noticeable degree, the basis upon which the U. S. Navy's present Law of Naval Warfare (NWIP 10-2) was promligated.   Although only Paragraphs (3), (4), and (12) of Part II, Second section of the 1916 Memorandum apply directly to the character of merchant shipping and non-commissioned auxiliaries, I feel that by taking out those particular paragraphs, the context of the overall Memorandum could be misinterpreted. One should study the entirety to obtain the comprehensive meaning. The Memorandum, beginning with Part I, Second Section follows. (Only the Prelude, earlier quoted, and the First Section of Part I which deals only with Armed Merchant Vessels in Neutral Ports have been omitted.)

"SECOND.--AN ARMED MERCHANT VESSEL ON THE HIGH SEAS

"(1) It is necessary for a belligerent warship to determine the status of an armed merchant vessel of an enemy encountered on the high seas, since the rights of life and property of belligerents and neutrals on board the vessel may be impaired if its status is that of an enemy warship.

"(2) The determination of warlike character must rest in no case upon presumption but upon conclusive evidence, because the responsibility for the destruction of life and property depends on the actual facts of the case and can not be avoided or lessened by a standard of evidence which a belligerent may announce as creating a presumption of hostile character. On the other hand, to safeguard himself from possible liability for unwarranted destruction of life and property the belligerent should, in the absence of conclusive evidence, act on the presumption that an armed merchantman is of peaceful character.

"(3) A presumption based solely on the presence of an armament on a merchant vessel of an enemy is not a sufficient reason for a belligerent to declare it to be a warship and proceed to attack it without regard to the rights of the persons on board. Conclusive evidence of a purpose to use the armament for aggression is essential. Consequently an armament which a neutral Government, seeking to perform its neutral duties, may presume to be intended for aggression, might in fact on the high seas be used solely for protection. A neutral Government has no opportunity to determine the purpose of an armament on a merchant vessel unless there is evidence in the ship's papers or other proof as to its previous use, so that the

Government is justified in substituting an arbitrary rule of presumption in arriving at the status of the merchant vessel. On the other hand, a belligerent warship can on the high seas test by actual experience the purpose of an armament on an enemy merchant vessel, and so determine by direct evidence the status of the vessel.

SUMMARY

"The status of an armed merchant vessel as a warship in neutral waters may be determined, in the absence of documentary proof or conclusive evidence of previous aggressive conduct, by presumption derived from all the circumstances of the case.

"The status of such vessel as a warship on the high seas must be determined only upon conclusive evidence of aggressive purpose, in the absence of which it is to be presumed that the vessel has a private and peaceable character and it should be so treated by an enemy warship.

"In brief, a neutral Government may proceed upon the presumption that an armed merchant vessel of belligerent nationality is armed for aggression, while a belligerent should proceed on the presumption that the vessel is armed for protection. Both of these presumptions may be overcome by evidence--the first by secondary or collateral evidence, since the fact to be established is negative in character; the second by primary and direct evidence, since the fact to be established is positive in character.

II

"The character of the evidence upon which the status of an armed merchant vessel of belligerent nationality is to be determined when visiting neutral waters and when traversing the high seas having been stated, it is important to consider the rights and duties of neutrals and belligerents as affected by the status of armed merchant vessels in neutral ports and on the high seas.

"FIRST.--THE RELATIONS OF BELLIGERENTS AND NEUTRALS AS AFFECTED BY THE STATUS OF ARMED MERCHANT VESSELS IN NEUTRAL PORTS

"(1) It appears to be the established rule of international law that warships of a belligerent may enter neutral ports and accept limited hospitality there upon condition that they leave, as a rule, within 24 hours after their arrival.

"(2)   Belligerent warships are also entitled to take on fuel once in three months in ports of a neutral country.

"(3)   As a mode of enforcing these rules a neutral has the right to cause belligerent warships failing to comply with them, together with their officers and crews, to be interned during the remainder of the war.

"(4)   Merchantmen of belligerent nationality, armed only for purposes of protection against the enemy, are entitled to enter and leave neutral ports without hinderance in the course of legitimate trade.

"(5)   Armed merchantmen of belligerent nationality under a commission or orders of their Government to use, under penalty, their armament for aggressive purposes, or merchantmen which, without such commission or orders, have used their armaments for aggressive purposes, are not entitled to the same hospitality in neutral ports as peaceable armed merchantmen.

"SECOND.--THE RELATIONS OF BELLIGERENTS AND NEUTRALS AS AFFECTED BY THE STATUS OF ARMED MERCHANT VESSELS ON THE HIGH SEAS.

"(1)   Innocent neutral property on the high seas can not legally be confiscated, but is subject to inspection by a belligerent. Resistance to inspection removes this immunity and subjects the property to condemnation by a prize court, which is charged with the preservation of the legal rights of the owners of neutral property.

"(2)   Neutral property engaged in contraband trade, breach of blockade, or unneutral service obtains the character of enemy property and is subject to seizure by a belligerent and condemnation by a prize court.

"(3)   When hostile and innocent property is mixed, as in the case of a neutral ship carrying a cargo which is entirely or partly contraband, this fact can only be determined by inspection. Such innocent property may be of uncertain character, as it has been frequently held that it is more or less contaminated by association with hostile property. For example, under the Declaration of London (which, so far as the provisions covering this subject are concerned, has been adopted by all the belligerents) the presence of a cargo, which in bulk or value consists of 50 per cent contraband articles, impresses the ship with enemy character and subjects it to seizure and condemnation by a prize court.

"(4)   Enemy   property,   including   ships   and cargoes, is always subject to seizure and condemnation. Any enemy property taken by a belligerent on the high seas is a total loss to the owners. There is no redress in a prize court. The only means of avoiding loss is by flight or successful resistance. Enemy merchant ships have, therefore,   the   right   to   arm   for   the   purpose   of self-protecton.

"(5)   A belligerent warship is any vessel which, under commission or orders of its Government imposing penalties or entitling it to prize money, is armed for the purpose of seeking and capturing or destroying enemy property or hostile neutral property on the seas. The size of the vessel, strength of armament, and its defensive or offensive force are immaterial.

"(6)   A belligerent warship has, incidental to the right of seizure, the right to visit and search all vessels on the high seas for the purpose of determining the hostile or innocent character of the vessel and their cargoes. If the hostile character of the property is known, however, the belligerent warship may seize the property without exercising the right of visit and search which is solely for the purpose of obtaining knowledge as to the character of the property. The attacking vessel must display its colors before exercising belligerent rights.

"(7)   When a belligerent warship meets a merchantman on the high seas which is known to be enemy owned and attempts to capture the vessel, the latter may exercise its right of self-protection either by flight or by resistance. The right to capture and the right to prevent capture are recognized as equally justifiable.

"(8)   The exercise of the right of capture is limited, nevertheless, by certain accepted rules of conduct based on the principles of humanity and regard for innocent property, even if there is definite knowledge that some of the property, cargo as well as the vessel, is of enemy character. As a consequence of these limitations, it has become the established practice for warships to give merchant vessels an opportunity to surrender or submit to visit and search before attempting to seize them by force. The observance of this rule of naval warfare tends to prevent the loss of life of noncombatants and the destruction of innocent neutral property which would result from sudden attack.

"(9) If, however, before a summons to surrender is given, a merchantman of belligerent nationality, aware of the approach of an enemy warship, uses its armament to keep the enemy at a distance, or after it has been summoned to surrender it resists or flees, the warship may properly exercise force to compel surrender.

"(10) If the merchantman finally surrenders, the belligerent warship may release it or take it into custody. In the case of an enemy merchantman it may be sunk, but only if it is impossible to take it into port, and provided always that the persons on board are put in a place of safety. In the case of a neutral merchantman, the right to sink it in any circumstance is doubtful.

"(11) A merchantman entitled to exercise the right of self-protection may do so when certain of attack by an enemy warship, otherwise the exercise of the right would be so restricted as to render it ineffectual. There is a distinct difference, however, between the exercise of the right of self-protection and the act of cruising the seas in an armed vessel for the purpose of attacking enemy naval vessels.

"(12) In the event that merchant ships of belligerent nationality are armed and under commission or orders to attack in all circumstances certain classes of enemy naval vessels for the purpose of destroying them, and are entitled to receive prize money for such service from their Government or are liable to a penalty for failure to obey the orders given, such merchant ships lose their status as peaceable merchant ships and are to a limited extent incorporated in the naval forces of their Government, even though it is not their sole occupation to conduct hostile operations.

"(13) A vessel engaged intermittently in commerce and under a commission or orders of its Government imposing a penalty, in pursuing and attacking enemy naval craft, possesses a status tainted with a hostile purpose which it can not throw aside or assume at will. It should, therefore, be considered as an armed public vessel and receive the treatment of a warship by an enemy and by neturals. Any person taking passage on such a vessel can not expect immunity other than that accorded persons who are on board a warship. A private vessel, engaged in seeking enemy naval craft, without such a commission or orders from its Government, stands in a relation to the enemy similar to that of a civilian who fires upon the organized military forces of a belligerent, and is entitled to no more considerate treatment."

When analyzing this 1916 Department of State document, it is clear that it contains the generalized understanding of International Law which was extant in 1914. The document then updates that understanding to coincide with the realities of modern sea warfare, circa 1916, and thus gives us the foundation for examination of certain classes of vessels and their actions during time of war.

For purposes of this study, I discuss only particular parts of the March 25, 1916, document. My comments reference the Memorandum by Part, Section and Paragraph and discuss the Memorandum's relevancy to both World War I and World War II.

I.   SECOND, ARMED MERCHANT VESSEL ON THE HIGH SEAS, SUMMARY (third paragraph)

Clearly the point is made here that "a belligerent should proceed on the presumption that [a] vessel is armed for protection," ie., defense. However, it also seems clear that such a presumption may be overcome by evidence. Thus it would appear that protective (defensive) armament is a connotation which is open to question if the gunners are subject, by governmental order, to use their guns offensively and under all circumstances. (Reference "The Relations of Belligerents as Effected by the Status of Armed Merchant Vessels...," Part II, Second; Paragraph [12]). The enemy's knowledge of the existence of an enforceable government order to initiate fire against the other side would seem to be appropriate evidence to overcome any presumption that the armament was protective (defensive) in nature.

II. SECOND Paragraph (3):

The quandry as to what legally identifies a ship as a contraband carrier was well covered under the provisions of the Declaration of London (1909) which described such a ship as having aboard a cargo consisting of at least 50% in bulk (or in value) of all such items being accordingly recognized as contraband. This concept has seemingly been incorporated within Paragraph 3. Even though it has become recognized that "class of cargo" no longer applies when defining contraband, the 50% formula can be useful in evaluating any vessel's contributory service toward its supportive role in the military war effort. This can also be useful in determining any ship's "Public Vessel" status whenever she is carrying mixed cargo, some part of which may have been consigned for government purposes with the remainder consigned into commercial trade. Accordingly, the 50% allowance, if exceeded, could be the factor to change the status of a merchantman to bring it under the laws and rules which apply to a "Public Vessel." (See Section this volume on Public Vessel Liability Act, its case law.)

II. SECOND Paragraph (4):

The right of a merchant vessel to arm is here made clear. The connotation is that such arming in and by itself is defensive and does not burden such ships with a change of character which might transform them into ships of war.

II. SECOND Paragraphs (8) and (10):

These paragraphs describe practices (circa 1916) which were derived by a long international understanding. They discuss the way that innocent and peaceable merchantmen are supposed to be treated by belligerents. The question, though, to be asked:

Was the merchant ship "innocent?"

II. SECOND Paragraph (12):

There are key phrases and words contained in this

paragraph   which   offer   us   definition   as   to   the
circumstances of Allied merchant seamen during either of
the World Wars.   For highlighted reference, those phrases
and words are here underlined followed by my comments on
each as given in brackets:

"In   the   event   merchant   ships   of   belligerent
nationality are armed and under commission or orders to
attack in all circumstances certain classes of enemy naval
vessels for the purpose of destroying them,..." [In World
War   I,   certain   restrictions   were   placed   regarding
initiating fire.   After our entry into World War II,
American merchant ship masters were under U. S. Naval
orders to fire on enemy submarines, aircraft, and surface
vessels; that fire was to be initiated immediately upon
identifying the enemy, and the gunners--both Navy and
merchantmen--were not to wait for the enemy to initiate
his own fire.]   "...and are entitled to receive prize
money for such service from their governments or are
liable to a penalty for failure to obey the orders
given..." [Masters and crewmen of the U. S. merchant
marine in World War II were subject to "penalty."
Following December 31, 1942, Naval orders and discipline
were applicable aboard U. S. merchant vessels once they
were upon the high seas; the masters (and crews) were

consequently, subject to court martial penalties as resulting from any conviction by Naval courts for disobedience to such orders;] ...such merchant ships lose their status as peaceable merchant ships and are to a limited extent incorporated in the naval forces of their Government, even though it is not their sole occupation to conduct hostile operations."

ARMING UNITED STATES MERCHANTMEN, WW I

On March 12, 1917, two weeks before the United States entered the European war, Robert Lansing, Secretary of the Department of State, announced that the United States had decided to place Naval Armed Guards on all American merchant ships sailing through areas which Germany had barred from commerce -- a blockade like prohibition which the United States refused to recognize. Lansing stated that the Naval Armed Guards were for the protection of the lives of the persons on board and for the safety of the vessel. Confidential instructions provided to the Master and the Armed Guard Commander were emphatic that the armament was, "for the sole purpose of defense against the unlawful acts of the submarines of Germany." Up to that time, Germany had already sunk eight American merchantmen which, at the time of attack, were within Germany's prohibited zone. On April 2, 1917, the United States Congress voted a Declaration of War against Germany. At that point, attacks by Germany against American shipping began in earnest.

It is the opinion of Government researchers, in

response to this author's requests for information, that the orders issued to the Naval Armed Guard in March 1917 remained virtually unchanged after hostilities began. [Conversation, Naval History Division, January, 1986.] There certainly was no "fire on sight" clause such as was contained in the British orders, nor were there any orders to "ram" such as were given to British shipmasters.

The instructions issued to the Armed Guard in March 1917 were entitled "REGULATIONS GOVERNING THE CONDUCT OF AMERICAN MERCHANT VESSELS ON WHICH NAVAL ARMED GUARDS HAVE BEEN PLACED" and were signed by Josephus Daniels, Secretary of the Navy. Paragraph 23 of these instructions placed the merchant master over the Armed Guard in all matters of non-military character. Paragraph 27 instructed that upon request of the Armed Guard commander, the Master was to detail members of the ship's crew "to supplement the service of the gun." Since certain provisions of the orders, namely Paragraphs 5) and 6) gave a "defensive" only connotation to the utilization of the armament, it is open to serious question as to whether these instructions had placed ordinary American merchant ships within the parameter of being "under orders to attack under all circumstances" during the period 1917-18. Officially, it would seem that the circumstances as brought about by the defensive Armed Guard restrictions

would have excluded World War I merchant ships from

Paragraph (12) of Part II, Second Section of the March 25,

1916, Memorandum.   In reality, though, one could be

critical of nit-picking on that point.   That which was

carried out in practice was what really mattered.   The

entire argument over "defensive" armament was properly put

into perspective during the 1922 Conference on the

Limitations of Armament held in Washington, DC.   As the

Advisory Committee for the United States delegation then

put it:

>   "The merchant ship sank the submarine if it came
> near enough;   the submarine sought and destroyed the
> merchant ship without even a knowledge of nationality or
> guilt...Defensive armament was almost sure to be used
> offensively in an attempt to strike a first blow."
> [Senate Doc. No. 126, 67th Congress, 2nd Session 1922,
> Wash. Conf. 274.]

# # #

> Note: One hundred twenty-six American merchant
> ships were lost through enemy action during World
> War I.   [MERCHANT VESSELS OF THE UNITED STATES,
> U. S. Department of Commerce, for the years 1917,
> 1918, 1919, and 1920.]

> The data I have to date collected is incomplete,
> however, I have so far determined that the Army
> Transport Service lost three ships to enemy
> action during the period 1917-18.   All were on
> bareboat charter to the Army, and all carried ATS
> crews.

THE MIXED CLAIMS COMMISSION

The Mixed Claims Commission which operated in the 1920s was an outgrowth of the provisions of the Treaty of Berlin, the impetus for which was the earlier Treaty of Versailles. The Commission's function was the issuance of rulings dealing with war reparations owed by Germany.

The Treaty of Berlin had been ratified by the U.S. Senate on the 14th of November 1921. Negotiations followed leading to an agreement between the United States and Germany regarding specific standards under which the Treaty provisions were to operate. The agreement called for two Commissioners, one from each nation, as well as an Umpire who was selected by concensus and who would decide any disagreement of the two Commissioners. Amended to the agreement were "Rules of Procedure." The prerequisite for claims to be made before the Commission was that

1.   damage to persons or property had to have been caused against an American national or American company by Germany during the active period of World War I.

2.   the damaged person, or company, was civilian in character.

The collateral from which the damage awards were
to be made was German property which was located in the
United States and which the United States Government had
seized in 1917 upon the outbreak of war with Germany. As
a direct result of the "Rules of Procedure," criteria was
developed by which the Commission could decide whether or
not claimants were legitimately civilian in character.
The Commission's deliberations and the criteria which it
subsequently developed are contained on Pages 75 through
101 REPORT OF THE MIXED CLAIMS COMMISSION - UNITED STATES
AND GERMANY, Administrative Decisions and Opinions of a
General Nature. When the Commission began developing the
specifics regarding U. S. merchant shipping which had been
sunk by Germany, it began by first arriving at the basis
of how a public vessel's employment could result in its
developing a military status.   In that regard the
Commission seems to have placed a considerable reliance on
the terms of the requisition charter form which, during
the two years of U. S. involvement in the war, had been
exercised by the U. S. Shipping Board whenever it took
over merchant shipping for Government use.   The
requisition charters stipulated that in "pending
emergencies" the ship could, on immediate

order, be used for the logistical support of the Army or
Navy; but when so doing, if it remained under the
management of the Agent operator (or agent owner) it
"shall not have the status of a Public Ship" but rather
would be subject to all the laws and regulations governing
merchant vessels.

> Note: Later, in 1919, the Supreme Court of the
> United States would uphold the legality of this
> provision by its judgment in the case of the LAKE
> MONROE [250 U. S. 246].

The requisition terms also specified that when a
vessel is "engaged in the service of the War or Navy
Department," meaning that its actual operation was
undertaken by one of those armed services, then in such a
case, the vessel shall have the status of a "Public Ship"
and that "the master, officers, and crew shall become the
immediate employees and agents of the United States with
all the rights and duties thereof."

The German representatives to the Commission
during the formulative conference stage had taken the
stand that any ship under United States ownership or
requisition, regardless of the service in which it would
be engaged, was "in furtherance of the U. S. war effort."
Therefore, they reasoned that in the absence of proof to
the contrary, it must be classed as "naval and military

works or materiels." The United States representatives
took a contrary view and did so with seemingly sound
justification. They counter argued that nothing short of
a ship's "operation by the United States directly in
furtherance of a military operation against Germany" could
have the effect of giving a ship a military or naval
character.

> Note: It should be mentioned that the argument
> taken by the United States representatives
> applied only to the Treaty of Versailles as that
> treaty was carried by reference into the Treaty
> of Berlin. (Versailles Treaty [para 9 of Annex I
> to Section I of Part VIII]). That provision
> stipulated that objects considered "Naval and
> military works or materiel" were not encompassed
> within the liability of reparations. Only
> damages to civilian works or materials were
> eligible for claims. It was therefore in the
> German interest to include as many things as they
> could under the category of "military." On the
> other hand, having more claims placed into the
> civilian category was far better from the United
> States's viewpoint.

The Commission decided that the phrase "Naval and
military words or materiel" as used in the Treaty "...had
no technical significance. It is not found in previous
treaties." The Commission also found that the phrase, in
whole or in part, was not a phrase previously construed,
either judicially or by administrative authority. They
concluded that the verbage was too vague for purposes of
administering claims. The United States's interpretation
was that when the phrase was applied to ships operated by

the United States, it should be taken to mean:

"[relating] solely to ships operated by the United States, not as merchantmen, but directly in furtherance of a military operation against Germany or her allies. A ship privately operated for private profit cannot be impressed with a military character, for only the government can lawfully engage in direct warlike activities."

The American representatives then went further by putting forth that the "true test" of a ship's status must be made based on the circumstances at the time that the damage occurred.

"Was the ship when destroyed being operated by the United States for purposes directly in furtherance of a military operation against Germany or her allies?" Ships being so operated were the only ones to be considered "as falling within the excepted military class and Germany is not obligated to pay the loss." If not so operated, it was not embraced within the excepted class, and Germany was, therefore, obligated to pay the loss. Since there were two American votes on the Commission to Germany's one, the United States's opinion of course was carried. The American dominated Commission then conceded, on Page 86 of the OPINIONS, that

'When, however, the Shipping Board delivered such vessels to either the War Department or the Navy Department of the United States, their status at once changed and they became public ships...and it was presumed that such delivery was made to the military arms of the Government to enable them to be used (in the language of Section 5 of the Shipping Act) 'as naval auxiliaries or Army transports, or for other naval or military purposes.' Such assignment of vessels to and their operations by the War Department or the Navy Department will be treated as prima facie but not conclusive evidence of their military character."

With the foundation now in place, the Commission subsequently drafted guidelines to be used in evaluating the case of each ship which would come before it:

"I. In order to bring a ship within the excepted class [military or naval character] she must have been operated by the United States at the time of her destruction for purposes directly in furtherance of a military operation against Germany or her allies.

"II. It is immaterial whether the ship was or was not owned by the United States; her possession, either actual or constructive, and her use by the United States in direct furtherance of a military operation against its then enemies constitutes the controlling test.

"III. So long as a ship is privately operated for private profit, she cannot be impressed with a military character, for only the Government can lawfully engage in warlike activities.

"IV. The fact that a ship was either owned or requisitioned by the Shipping Board, or the Fleet Corporation, and operated by one of them, either directly or through an agent, does not create even a rebuttable presumption that she was impressed with a military character.

"V. When, however, a ship either owned by or requisitioned by the United States during the period of belligerency passed into the possession and under the operation of either the War Department or the Navy Department of the United States, thereby becoming a public ship, her master, officers, and crew all being employed and paid by and subject to the orders of the United States, it is to be presumed that such possession, control, and operation by a military arm of the government focusing all of its powers and energies on actively waging war, were directly in furtherance of a military operation. Such control and operation of a ship will be treated by the Commission as prima facie, but not conclusive evidence of her military character.

'VI.   Neither (a) the arming for defensive purposes of a merchantman, nor (b) the manning of such armament by a naval gun crew, nor (c) her routing by the Navy Department of the United States for the purposes of avoiding the enemy, nor (d) the following by the civilian master of such merchantman of instructions given by the Navy Department for the defense of the ship when attacked by or when in danger of attack by the enemy, nor, (e) her seeking the protection of a convoy and submitting herself to naval instruction as to route and operation for the purpose of avoiding the enemy, or all these combined, will not suffice to impress such merchantmen with a military character.

'VII.   The facts in each case will be carefully examined and weighed and the Commission will determine whether or not the particular ship at the time of her destruction was operated by the United States directly in furtherance of a military operation against Germany or her allies.   If she was so operated, she will fall within the excepted class, otherwise she will not."

Thirteen cases were initially reviewed on a test basis as an aid in establishing criteria.   Ten of them were deemed to be merchant ships; by falling outside of the excepted class, they were eligible for damage claims to be payable out of the seized German properties.   Those ten ships are listed here along with the activity that each was engaged in at the time of the loss.   The three other ships were deemed to fall within the excepted class, i.e., having military character.   In consequence, they were not eligible for judgments of damage.   The three within the excepted class were all Army Transports, manned by civil Service crews. 4

MERCHANT SHIPS -- (CIVILIAN CHARACTER)

(Tanker) MONTANO: Lost July 31, 1917; privately owned and operated; military cargo; armed; merchant crew

SS PINAR DE RIO: Lost June 8, 1918; requisitioned by U.S.; time chartered to agent; Commercial cargo; unarmed; merchant crew

SS ROCHESTER: Lost Nov 2, 1917; privately owned and operated; commercial cargo; armed; merchant crew

(Tanker) MORENI: Lost June 12, 1917; privately owned and operated; commercial cargo; armed; merchant crew

SS ALMANCE: Lost Feb 5, 1918; requisitioned by U.S., under agency management for U.S.; commercial cargo; armed; merchant crew

SS TYLER: Lost April 13, 1918; requisitioned by U.S., under agency management for U.S.; commercial cargo; armed; merchant crew

SS SANTA MARIA: Lost Feb 25, 1918; requisitioned by U.S., under agency management for U.S.; commercial cargo; armed; merchant crew

SS MERAK: Lost Aug 6, 1918; requisitioned by U.S., under agency management for U.S.; commercial cargo; unarmed; merchant crew

SS TEXEL: Lost June 2, 1918; requisitioned by U.S., under agency management for U.S.; commercial cargo; unarmed; merchant crew

MILITARY AUXILIARIES - (MILITARY CHARACTER)

USAT JOHN G. McCULLOUGH: Lost May 18, 1918; requisitioned
                    by U. S. and chartered to War
                    Department; military cargo; armed;
                    Civil Service crew

(Tanker) USAT JOSEPH CUDAHY: Lost Aug 17 1918;
                    requisitioned by U. S. and chartered to
                    War Department; military cargo; armed;
                    Civil Service crew

USAT A. A. RAVEN: Lost March 14, 1918; requisitioned by
                   U. S. and chartered to War Department;
                   military cargo; armed; Civil Service
                   crew

MIXED CLAIMS COMMISSION OPINIONS

--An Appraisal--

Overall, the Commission seems to have followed a line of precedent in international legal standards when judging the thirteen test cases. Its understanding of "Public Ship" seems proper in light of the situation as it existed in 1917-18. I would agree with the Commission that under the arrangement by which the ten merchant ships were operated, it is difficult to attach a direct military support significance to any of them. Even though the tanker MONTANO was carrying Admiralty consigned oil, she was not under Government charter or control, and her owner, the Standard Oil Company of New Jersey, undertook that voyage for profit. It is difficult therefore to argue that she could be brought out from under the meaning of the term "merchantman" even though her voyage was undertaken in support of a military operation.

There is a further question regarding the seven merchant ships which were armed. Did this give them a military significance? Mallison, writing in 1966, discussed the aspect of integration into the military by the arming of merchant ships in the 1914-18 war. He

questions the Mixed Claims Commission's decisions as they

related to International Law--at least as Mallison

believed it should have been understood at that time.

> "As a belligerent, the United States helped the
> United Kingdom to perfect the merchant ship as an
> effective combatant unit. The United States, like the
> United Kingdom, armed its merchant ships and sailed them
> in convoys escorted by naval vessels. In addition, the
> United States exercised comprehensive government control
> over the voyage sailed and the cargoes carried by merchant
> shipping to insure that it was employed in the most
> efficient manner possible on behalf of the war effort."
> [Mallison, Page 113.]

Further examining the United States policy of

arming its merchant ships, Footnote 83 of Mallison's cites

Savage's POLICY OF THE UNITED STATES TOWARD MARITIME

COMMERCE IN WAR. On Page 582, Savage had reproduced a

U.S. Naval order of March 13, 1917, establishing the

operational procedures to be followed by Naval Armed Guard

Commanders and merchant ship masters whenever making

contact with German submarines. These orders predated by

nineteen days the United States entry into hostilities and

therefore addressed the then neutral policy taken by the

United States whenever one of its armed merchant ships was

to encounter a German submarine on the high seas.

> "...no Armed Guard on any merchant vessel shall take any
> offensive action against any submarine of Germany or of
> any nation following the policy of Germany announced in
> her note of January 17, 1917, on the high seas outside of
> the zones prescribed by Germany, unless the submarine is

guilty of an unlawful act that jeopardizes the vessel, her
passengers or crew, or unless the submarine is submerged."

The order, further stipulated:

"No armed guard on an American merchant vessel shall
attack a submarine that is retiring or attempting to
retire either within or without a zone prescribed by
Germany, unless it may be reasonably presumed to be
maneuvering for renewal of attack."

Obviously, when the United States entered the war
as a belligerent, those parts of the orders dealing with
the cessation of fire whenever a submarine was retiring
into or out of "a zone prescribed by Germany" were no
longer to be applied. However, the prohibition against
taking offensive action against a submarine -- the part of
the order not to initiate fire against the submarine --
does not appear to have been rescinded. At least as I
have earlier brought out in this study, no change in this
order to Armed Guards followed March of 1917. If this is
truly the case, then American merchant ships circa 1917-18
could be considered to have been under orders to use their
guns in the defensive sense only. Defensively armed
vessels would therefore not have been imbued with a naval
combatant function under any technical understanding of
International Law either circa 1917-18 or to this day.

Note: As stated earlier, though, how the
armament was actually used would have been a
truer test than the technical content of the
order.

I tend to question Dr. Mallison's contention that the U.S. merchant marine of 1917-18 was under "comprehensive government control over the voyages sailed and the cargoes carried." True, the Government had requisition power which it exercised over a fairly wide spectrum; however, whenever ships were time chartered back to commercial operators, then the Government control (unlike the case of World War II) was greatly diluted. The mobilization of shipping space for all out war purposes was no where near as great in 1917-18 as it was in World War II. Using the examples of the ten merchant ship cases selected for study by the Mixed Claims Commission, only five had voyage descriptions which would fit the criteria for being under full operational Government control. The other five were under the operational control of their owners or Agents, even though their exact routing orders may have been provided by Naval authority.

When applying the Commission's opinions to identify the status of crewmembers aboard vessels having military character, I found it helpful to review Commission case histories which pertained generally to civilians working in conjunction with military forces engaged in operation against the enemy. Such opinions are

useful, not only in analyzing the case of World War I, but
also in providing an understanding of certain civilian
employment during World War II and even beyond that, to
the present day. Commission case Docket 4259 deals with
civilians assimilated into the support of active military
operations, with the proviso that they are in the employ
and under the control of a recognized military
organization.

"...The line of demarcation between the 'civilian
population' and the military within the meaning of the
Treaty [Treaty of Versailles, carried over into the Treaty
of Berlin] is not an arbitrary line drawn by the statutory
enactments of the nation, each nation drawing it in a
different place, but a natural line determined by the
occupation at the time of the injury or damage complained
of, of the individual national of the Allied and
Associated Powers, without reference to the particular
nation to which he may have happened to belong. An
individual who is wholly in the employ and control of the
army of an Allied and Associated Power and is immediately
engaged in a work directly in furtherance of a military
operation against Germany, cannot at the time be treated
as a part of the 'civilian population' of the nation to
which he belongs, although he may not be nominally
enrolled in the military organization of that nation so as
to have a 'military status' for all purposes effecting the
domestic relation between him and his government."
        [MIXED CLAIMS COMMISSION, U. S. AND GERMANY,
ADMINISTRATIVE DECISIONS AND OPINIONS OF A GENERAL
NATURE...to June 30, 1925. Specific cases:
        Christian Damson, United States v. Germany,
Docket 4259, Decisions and Opinions, 1925-26, 242, 259-263.
        Arthur Elliot Hungerford, ante, pp 173-174.]

POST WORLD WAR I LEGISLATION

Following World War I, four important legislative events occurred which help us in defining when the term "merchant vessel" no longer is applicable and at what point a ship takes on another character.

The four major legislative events were:

THE MERCHANT MARINE ACT OF 1920 [Title 46 USCA, Chapter 24]

THE MERCHANT MARINE ACT OF 1936 [Title 46 USCA, Chapter 27]

THE PUBLIC VESSEL LIABILITY ACT [Title 46 USCA, Chapter 22 as passed March 3, 1925]

INSPECTION OF STEAM VESSELS (Revision) [Title 46, USCA, Chapter 14]

The Merchant Marine Acts

The Merchant Marine Acts of 1920 and 1936 have, within their preambles, a reiteration of the purpose of the 1916 Shipping Act in that the mission of the merchant marine in peace is to carry the nation's commerce; and in war to serve as "a naval and military auxiliary." 5 Under a provision of the 1936 Act [Title 46, USCA §1242] the government, in times of emergencies and for purposes of national defense, is given the authority to requisition, by charter or other means, the individual merchant vessels of the United States. The stage was therefore set for what became a nearly complete nationalization of the U. S. merchant fleet during World War II. During that conflict, the U.S. merchant fleet would lose its commercial character to become a logistical sea arm for a nation which was mobilized for all-out war, a war which was conducted on all of the world's continents, including, in one isolated incident, the continent of Antarctica.

The Public Vessel Liability Act

The Public Vessel Liability Act of 1925 resulted in case history dealing with refinement of the term "public vessel" in its recitement by the courts. [Note 15 of Title 46, Chapter 22 §781 USCA.]

"Government ownership and use of a vessel in manner directed by the government exclusively for public purpose would suffice without more to make ship a public vessel within this chapter. Petition of U. S., C. A. Del 1966."

"A vessel bound for port in United States with coal belonging to Army where she was to complete her cargo by loading munitions of war after which she was to sail for the European Theater of War was not a 'merchant vessel' within section 742 of this Title but was a 'public vessel' within the section, and negligence of such vessel in a United States port resulting in death of fireman on destroyer did not give rise to action for damages against United States. Bradey v. U. S., C.C.A. NY 1945."

"Whether a ship is a 'public' or 'merchant' vessel must be determined by reference to the nature of the services she rendered and the nature of the services should be determined by looking to the specific service being rendered at the time the asserted claim arose. Petition of Oskar Tiedmann and Company, D.C., Del 1964."

"A vessel not only owned by the United States but engaged in a defense activity at time it was involved in an accident giving rise to claims for injury and wrongful deaths of seamen would be regarded as a 'public vessel' for purposes of denying an award of prejudgment interest against the United States, and the vessel could not be classed as a 'merchant vessel' even though she had a civilian crew and even though the United States was not at war at time the collision occurred. Id."

"The charter party test for determining whether a vessel is a public vessel or a merchant vessel is restricted in its application to a privately owned vessel carrying public cargo, because it is by resort to terms of charter party that court is able to decide nature of government's interest in privately owned vessel and extent of control exercised by government over such vessel at a given time. Geo. W. Rogers Const. Corps. v U.S., D. C. N.Y. 1954."

"A vessel owned absolutely by United States through Maritime Commission and operated by officers who are civil service employees of United States and by crew paid by United States through its general agent is a public vessel within purview of this chapter, unless it is engaged in transporting cargo for hire for private shippers. Id."

"A vessel under control of United States Navy and used for transportation of personnel and military supplies is a 'public vessel' within purview of this chapter. Roeper v U. S., DCNY 1949."

Under Note 38:
"In libel for wages by civilian seamen against United States, exceptive allegations that vessels on which seaman was employed were operated by Army Transportation Service, Transportation Corps, United States Army, an agency of the War Department and were public vessels of the United States were assumed to be facts which should be judicially noticed in absence of objection. Jentry v U. S. D. C. Cal. 1947."

Inspection of Steam Vessels

The law dealing with the inspection of steam vessels was amended on October 25, 1919 [c. 82, 41 Stat. 35]. This amendment brought "public vessels" (other than those owned or under the demise control of the Army or Navy) under the full umbrella of controls exercised under the U. S. Navigation and Inspection Laws.

BIRMINGHAM CITY. "Hog Island" class freighter. Torpedoed and sunk off Dutch Guiana during January of 1943. (Courtesy A. Moore)

T-2 class tanker armed with one 5″ gun; one 3″ gun; six 20-mm cannon. (Courtesy A. Moore)

Liberty ship dockside unloading military cargo at an overseas port. (WSA photo)

Some of the "sophisticated" weaponry (30 calibre "Lewis guns") provided to U.S. merchant ships in 1942. Scene was bow of SS MEANTICUT, a ship under charter to War Shipping Administration. Photo was taken following action against German aircraft, Barents Sea. (Courtesy B. Brigadier)

20-mm gun tubs mounted aboard "Hog Island" class freighter. Note how lifeboat is swung out ready for abandoning ship if that should become necessary. This ship and her crew survived. Many others did not. (Courtesy B. Brigadier)

Merchant crew loading 20-mm shells into magazines, Convoy PQ-18. At the time this photo was taken ammunition supply was running low and crew was contemplating invading the cargo for a fresh supply. (Courtesy B. Brigadier)

Some of the merchant crew, SS MEANTICUT. On voyage to northern Russia; Convoy PQ-18, 1942. Note age differences of the men. (Courtesy B. Brigadier)

German bomber coming in low moments before it was shot down. Convoy PQ-18 to north Russia, 1942. (Courtesy B. Brigadier)

Near miss! Aerial attack, Barents Sea, 1942. (Courtesy B. Brigadier)

Bomb hit on munitions ship. No survivors. Convoy PQ-18. (Courtesy B. Brigadier)

PART II

- WORLD WAR II -

THE REARMING OF MERCHANT SHIPS AND AUXILIARIES

The United States Neutrality Act of 1939, Section 6, prohibited the arming of American merchant vessels during the existence of a proclamation of a state of war between foreign states. Later, Section 2 of the Act of 17 November 1941 (55 Stat 864) repealed Section 6 of the 1939 Neutrality Act, thus removing the prohibition against armaments on vessels of the merchant marine.

> Note: There was never a prohibition under the Neutrality Act (or) any other U.S. statute against the armament of naval or military auxiliaries. It was not, however, a part of the internal program of the War Department to arm Army Transports during time of peace.

It was not U. S. policy to allow private ship owners to arm their own vessels; rather, the guns, their installations, and the cadre for the gun crews was to become the direct responsibility of the Navy Department. Merchant crews would be assigned to gun stations to act as assistants in support of the Naval cadres.

The first Naval Armed Guard unit to board a U. S. merchant ship was assigned to the SS DUNBOYNE on December 1, 1941, (six days before Pearl Harbor.) The instructions issued by the Navy to merchant vessels were first drafted

in 1940 by Chief of Naval Operations, Division of Fleet
Training. These were issued in entirety to all U. S.
merchant vessels carrying armament and stood as standard
procedure until modified through changes beginning in
1942. The original orders -- less Confidential elements
-- were also reprinted within the MERCHANT MARINE OFFICERS
HANDBOOK, Turpen and McEwen, Cornell Maritime Press. The
instructions of 1940 were entitled "NAVAL TRANSPORTATION
AND OPERATION OF MERCHANT VESSELS IN TIME OF WAR."
Following is one section of those instructions, the
subtitle being "Conditions Under Which Fire May Be Opened."

"Against an enemy acting in accordance with
International Law. As the armament is solely for the
purpose of self-defense, it must only be used against an
enemy who is clearly attempting to capture or sink the
merchant ship. On the outbreak of war it should be
assumed that the enemy will act in accordance with
International Law, and fire should therefore not be opened
until he has made it plain that he intends to attempt
capture. Once it is clear that resistance will be
necessary if capture is to be averted, fire should be
opened immediately.

"Against an enemy acting in defiance of
International Law. If, as the war progresses, it
unfortunately becomes clear that, in defiance of
International Law, the enemy has adopted a policy of
attacking merchant ships without warning, it will then be
permissible to open fire on an enemy surface vessel,
submarine or aircraft, even before she has attacked or
demanded surrender, if to do so will tend to prevent her
gaining a favorable position for attacking.

"Before opening fire, United States colors must
be hoisted."

Forty-five years after they were authored, there
is some skepticism which goes with the reading of these
instructions. Heralded throughout is reference to

"Defensive Armament;" a phrasing that the the armament was for "defensive purposes only," etc. Yet, the history of World War II tells us that by the time the orders were drafted and well before they were issued (1941), Germany had launched into full unrestricted warfare. By 1941, only the second paragraph of the above could have applied. Obviously, the SS DUNBOYN's gunners were to deal with an enemy "acting in defiance of International Law." The passive action of waiting to be fired upon before opening fire was not to be a factor for consideration. The instructions continued on to cover a wide gamut of situations and even included some assurances:

"Non-Combatant Status
        "By using force to resist capture, a ship does not lose her noncombatant status. There is a distinct difference between the exercise of the right of self protection and the act of cruising the high seas in an armed vessel for the purpose of attacking enemy vessels."

Taken as is, the above is correct; however, it totally ignored the order covering the merchant ship's role to be taken "Against an enemy acting in defiance of International Law," whereby the merchant ship was ordered to open fire before she herself is attacked. It also ignored the almost certain pending state of war. Predetermined policy of the United States Navy had established that during war, Naval Law would be exercised over the civilians of the U.S. merchant marine. It is logically presumed that those who issued the instructions in late 1941 were cognizant of both of these factors. The Office of the Chief of Naval Operations was certainly aware that it would be but a matter of time before Naval discipline would be imposed over the merchant marine.

In 1937, Naval Courts and Boards had ruled:

"The officers, members of crews, and passengers on board merchant ships of the United States, although not in the Naval Service of the United States, are, under the laws of the United States, decisions of the courts, and by the necessity of the case, subject to military control while in the actual theater of war."

As of December 31, 1942, the Navy ruled that

"All waters outside the territorial waters of neutral and unoccupied countries have been declared to be a 'zone of military operations.'"

[Commandant, Twelfth Naval District, to Masters of all Merchant Vessels, 31 December 1942, P13-9, (34073-14-B/Sk, signed by J. W. Greenslade.]

Following December 31, 1942, the circumstance of merchant seamen serving aboard armed ships with Naval Armed Guards was that once detailed to a gun station by the ship's master, the merchant crewman then came under the orders (and discipline) of the Armed Guard officer while at those gun stations. A seaman was part and parcel of the ship's naval fighting force. Was he still, as the 1941 Naval orders would have led him to believe, just a harmless civilian defending his ship? Hardly. It seems quite apparent that the draftors of the 1940 Naval order

issued in 1941 were aware even then that merchant seamen

assigned as part of Naval gun crews and operating under

Naval orders would lose their civilian status under

International Law.

> "126   Participation in armed resistance must be
> confined to persons acting under the orders of the Master
> or officer in command of the armed guard. Passengers who
> are not members of the naval or military services should
> not participate in an actual engagement with the enemy,
> but there is no objection to such persons acting as
> lookouts." [Naval Instructions; Section 8, Paragraph 126,
> 1940, Navy Department]

> "Only individuals who have lawful combatant
> status are entitled to exercise violence during war or
> hostilities....Such individuals, upon capture by the
> enemy, are to be accorded the standards of treatment
> prescribed by international law for prisoners of
> war....Unlawful combatants who are captured enjoy
> considerably less protection under law." [Mallison, Pg 10]

The military control which was extended over

merchant crews through the Naval Courts and Boards ruling

of 1937 and which was completed later with the geographic

establishment of that control through the December 31,

1942 ruling had fully integrated these merchant seamen or

armed ships with the Naval force.

As to other civilians who might be aboard

merchant ships as passengers, their status was somewhat

different. The Naval gunnery instructions, Paragraph 126,

recognized this. But what of those pasengers? Could they

expect immunity from personal harm?

"It is lawful to kill or wound enemy combatants, that is naval or merchant marine personnel, pursuant to a lawful attack upon an enemy warship or merchant ship. During such an attack, it is not only lawful to kill or wound the combatant personnel, but it is also lawful to kill or wound the otherwise especially protected medical and religious personnel incidental to attack on the ship." [Mallison, Pages 132-33]

Drawing on the experience of World War II, the U. S. Navy has drawn a specific distinction between combatants and noncombatants. The following quotation is taken from LAW OF NAVAL WARFARE, NWIP 10-2, Department of Navy, Office of the Chief of Naval Operations, September 1955, (Article 221, Page 2-4).

"a)   Distinction. The traditional laws of war are based largely on the distinction made between combatants and noncombatants. In accordance with the distinction, the population of a belligerent is divided into two general classes: the armed forces (combatants) and the civilian population (noncombatants). Each class has specific duties and rights in time of war and no person can belong to both classes at the same time."

NWIP 10-2, Chapter 2, Footnote 10 amplifies this:

"10   The terms 'civilian population' and 'noncombatants' are used interchangeably in Article 221 and refer to those peaceful inhabitants of a State who neither are attached to or accompany the armed forces. It should be observed that the term 'noncombatants' also has a more restricted meaning and refers to certain categories of individuals who are attached to or accompany the armed forces of a belligerent, eg. hospital personnel, chaplains, correspondents, etc. The status of these noncombatant categories is dealt with in the detailed provisions of the 1949 Geneva Conventions for the Protection of Victims of War."

[Note: Red Cross workers are also protected as noncombatants under successive International Conventions including Geneva, 1949; Article 63 of that Convention.]

The situation for armed merchant ships following December 31, 1942, had become simply this:

*   The ships were now clearly combatant in character.

*   The merchant crews and naval gunners taken together and as individuals constituted a lawful combatant force since collectively and individually they were operating under the orders of their government.

*   Noncombatant personnel, ie., civilian passengers, war correspondents, Red Cross workers, medical and religious personnel, were subject to the same unrestricted and unwarned attack as were the merchant crews and naval gunners since essentially the enemy when coming upon an armed merchant vessel, legitimately identified all aboard her with the character of the ship. There is a distinct and quite obvious difference between naval war and land war, namely the difficulty in sea or air war in separating the individual's identification from that of his ship or aircraft.

"The uniform is regarded as more important in land than in naval or air war." [Mallision, Footnote 3, Page 29]

Only when personnel aboard the ship were taken captive could they be identified so that any distinction could clearly be made. The provisions which are now found within the LAW OF NAVAL WARFARE NWIP 10-2 (1955) are generally the same as those followed by the belligerents in World War II. For instance, Article 512 of NWIP 10-2 states, "The Officers and crews of captured merchantmen may be made prisoners of war." Footnote 37 of Chapter 5 of NWIP 10-2 reads:

"However the general practice of belligerents during World

War I and World War II was to treat the officers and crews of all captured enemy merchant vessels as prisoners of war."

One major misunderstanding over the status of merchant marine personnel in World War II has been the direct relationship of their combatant status to their ship. For instance, a merchant seaman found ashore without attachment to a ship is the same as any other noncombatant civilian. In this respect, he is quite different than a member of a uniformed armed force. This was even recognized by the Japanese in their handling of certain American and British merchant seamen who were without shipboard employment, being ashore in Manila at the time of the city's capture. These men were, in most instances, handled as civilian internees rather than as prisoners of war. Those captured at sea by the Japanese were almost always handled as prisoners of war.

Note: A member of the U.S. Armed Forces is generally under a "term contract" known as an enlistment or, in the case of officers, a contractual period. (In World War II, this was generally for the "period of hostilities and six months thereafter.") In the case of U.S. merchant seamen, their contract was in the form of Shipping Articles entered into for service upon a specific ship for a stated term or voyage. At the time he was discharged from the ship, he was released from the obligations of those Articles, therefore, becoming an unemployed civilian until such time that he joined another ship by signing that ship's Articles.

The arming of merchant ships in the war's early days was not universal owing to a lack of available guns and the necessary time required to train Naval gun crews. However, by the late summer of 1942, most merchant and public ships were armed; and most, but not all, carried at least a partial complement of guns and Naval gunners.

While the Navy was busy training its Armed Guards, the U. S. Maritime Commission (upon request via the Chief of Naval Operations as dated 22 December 1941) undertook, in cooperation with the British, the gunnery training of American merchant seamen whose ships touched at British ports. Both American merchant seamen and Naval Armed Guard attended those British schools. Later, dockside training areas were established by the United States Navy at domestic ports to accomodate attendance by both naval gunners and merchant seamen. The merchant marine system of signing on and off Shipping Articles at the beginning and end of each voyage did not foster heavy attendance at the schools by off-duty merchant seamen whose primary interest between voyages centered on assorted modes of rest and relaxation, none of which included gunnery. A system to establish well attended gunnery training was instituted by including gunnery courses at Maritime Commission training facilities.

Note: Gunnery as a subject was taught at the maritime officer training schools which were operated by the Army Transportation Corps at St. Petersburg, Florida, and at New Orleans. On smaller auxiliary vessels (those less than 1000 tons) which carried guns but which did not have sufficient accommodations for gun crews, those officers who had previously been trained at the Army's cadet schools conducted basic gunnery instruction for all vessel's personnel.

The Navy's standard arrangement starting in 1941 with the issuance of the Instructions of 1940 and continuing with successive amended orders (1942, 1943, 1944, 1945) was that the ship's master was to supply members of his merchant crew to serve as ammunition handlers. In addition, he was to supply five assistant gunnery personnel for each 5" gun; three for each 4" gun and 3" gun; and two for lesser calibers. Additionally, two assistant gunners were to come from the merchant crew for each 20 mm gun, and one assistant gunner was to be supplied for each 50 caliber machine gun.

[OPERATIONS REGULATIONS No. 35, January 25, 1943, War Shipping Administration, pages 2, 3.]

[GENERAL INSTRUCTIONS FOR COMMANDING OFFICERS OF NAVAL ARMED GUARD ON MERCHANT SHIPS, 4th Edition (OPNAV 23L-2) 1944 ¶5803]

Note: The average liberty ship or T-2 tanker (1944) had a merchant marine crew of 37 officers and men. Both classes of ships were generally supplied with one 5" gun; one 3" gun; and six 20-mm anti-aircraft cannons. With such armament and according to the Navy and WSA instructions to the masters, this meant that sixteen members of the merchant crew were assigned as assistant

gunners. To operate a liberty or T-2 tanker --
meaning the mere act of keeping it steaming ahead
-- required at least nine men, including the
master. This left a remainder of only twelve of
the merchant crew to act as ammunition handlers.
It is apparent then that during times of
engagement with the enemy, when crews were at
battle stations, the entire merchant marine
complement was actively engaged in either running
the vessel or carrying out gunnery assignments.

Additional battle Instructions issued in
1942 to merchant ships at the beginning of the war
are contained in a pamphlet entitled AXIS SUBMARINE
MANUAL, Office of Naval Intelligence (ONI 220-M),
reference OP-16-F-20/SS EF74/Serial No. 3849016.
This was distributed to "masters and seamen of our
merchant marine and for armed guard crews."
Paragraph (46) contains instructions which included
methods for ramming the enemy whenever applicable and
without waiting to be first attacked. The Archives
contain voluminous documents called OPNAVS issued to
merchant masters and Armed Guard officers, these
spell out the wartime combined gunnery duties of both
the Naval Armed Guard and the merchant crews. Such
documents are identified as: OP-23-L-McC,
S0116-1037, Serial 459123 dated Nov 6, 1942, signed
by Newton acting for CNO; Bulletin #28, File No.
A16-3/ESE II signed by Adolphus Andrews, V. Adm.;
OPNAV 23L-2, 1944. Scuttling instructions addressed

to ships masters were received through Navy orders
OP23-JH (SC) S76-3 Ser. 097923 dated March 30, 1942.

The early-on relationship between civilian
masters and Navy gunnery officers often times left
some room for command confusion between the parties.
The Navy clarified this problem:

"command of the ship under all circumstances is vested
entirely in the civilian master."

That instruction was contained in Naval orders and was
also incorporated, by reference, to Army Transports within
Army Regulation AR 55-330, Par 5, 1 December 1942.

[U. S. ARMY IN WORLD WAR II, The Technical Series,
Transportation Corps Responsibilities, Organization, and
Operation; Chester Wardlow; Office of the Chief of
Military History, Washington 1951, p. 246]

The Navy OPNAV recognized the master's authority over the
Navy gunners in respect to their general conduct, dress,
and permission to go ashore. The Armed Guard commander
retained the direct control of military discipline over
his gunnery detachment. (After December 1942, that
discipline applied to merchant seamen while assigned to
gunnery stations.) The OPNAV specified the Armed Guard
Commander's authority to open fire on the enemy on his own
initiative, although orders to commence an action could
initiate from the master as well. According to Wardlow,

the Navy informally recognized that for extreme
disciplinary cases, the master, in view of his paramount
command position, was justified in arresting and confining
members, including officer, of the Armed Guard. This
responsibility was vested under the overall control given
the master under the Navigation Laws (Title 46).

In those circumstances where the master of a
merchant ship required the exercise of military control
over either his crew or passengers, he had the legal
option to call upon the Commander of the Armed Guard to
assist in implementing that discipline.

The Navy gunners and the civilian seamen became a
synchronized team although on some ships, friction did
develop between the factions. 6 One example of exemplary
team work on the part of both merchant and Navy in action
against the enemy is the story of the STEPHEN HOPKINS, a
liberty ship -- the only American surface ship (naval or
merchant) to have sunk a German naval ship of any
significance. The engagement took place in the South
Atlantic between the STEPHEN HOPKINS and the German raider
STIER which at the time was in company with the supply
ship TANNENFELS. The STIER was sunk as was the STEPHEN
HOPKINS.

"A final comprehensive tribute to all who served
on the STEPHEN HOPKINS during her great fight was paid in

the words of a spokesman for the Office of the Chief of Naval Operations:

"'The extraordinary heroism and outstanding devotion to duty of the officers and crew of the Armed Guard and the ship's company were in keeping with the highest tradition of American seamanship. Their fearless determination to fight their ship and perserverance to engage the enemy to the utmost until their ship was rendered useless, aflame, and in a sinking condition, demonstrated conduct beyond the call of duty.'"

[A CARELESS WORD...A NEEDLESS SINKING by Captain Arthur R. Moore, United States Merchant Marine Academy Museum, Kings Point, NY, Page 270.]

Intelligence Gathering

Intelligence gathering by both merchant ships and Army Transports was standard procedure during World War II. Ships were under naval orders to break radio silence upon the approach of a suspected enemy vessel in order to disclose the enemy's location to Allied Naval forces.

Merchant masters were expected to cooperate in reporting to Naval and military authorities the state of conditions in designated ports of call which were not under U. S. or Allied jurisdiction. This latter task was accomplished through the filing of reports to both naval and military intelligence branches.

[Ship Files, Second Drawer, Cabinet 16, Mr. Larson's Files, Stack No. 3, National Records Center, Suitland, Maryland]

[Navy Instructions, per Section 142 as reprinted in MERCHANT MARINE OFFICERS HANDBOOK, Cornell Maritime Press, 1943.]

"The reference to merchant ships in the Protocol [London Naval Protocol of 1930] could with consistency, have been interpreted as not applicable to any vessel including neutrals, so integrated into the British [or American] warning network." [Mallison, Pages 80, 81]

Mallison's belief is substantiated by no less than the "Committee of Jurists" who participated in the drafting of the London Protocol. Their report issued April 3, 1930, said,

"The Committee wishes it to be placed on record that the expression 'merchant vessel' where it is employed in the declaration, is not to be understood as including a merchant vessel which is at the moment participating in hostilities in such a manner as to cause her to lose her right to the immunitites of a merchant vessel."

[Department of State Proceedings of the London Naval Conference of 1930 and Supplementary Documents (Conference Series No. 6, 1931.)]

State Department Policy, 1941-45

During the period 1941 through 1945, the U. S. Department of State, as far as I can determine through a search of Department position papers, made nothing in the way of any statement which could be regarded as an alteration in policy from its long established viewpoint over armed merchant ships or to the status of the crews of

such ships. The closest the Department came to such a
change between 1941 and 1945 was more in the way of an
updating through the writings of Green Haywood Hackworth,
Legal Advisor to the Department of State. Hackworth's
writings in 1943 within a Department publication dealt
with the Department's position earlier taken in the white
paper of March 25, 1916, part of which is reproduced
earlier in this treatise.

On his page 498, Hackworth quotes from a note
President Wilson wrote to Secretary of State Lansing on
January 31, 1917, in which Wilson made pointed reference
to the British practice of ordering its merchant masters
to initiate fire against German submarines.

"...that the British are going beyond the spirit at any
rate, of the principles hitherto settled in regard to this
matter and that the method in which their ship captains
are instructed to use their guns has in many instances
gone beyond what could legitimately be called defense. It
appears that they have more than once attacked. The
question is more whether their guns have been used only
for defense than whether they exceed in calibre what would
reasonably constitute armament for defense and whether
their being mounted in the bow is a presumption that they
are being used for offense."

There is no instance within Hackworth's 1943
paper where he takes exception to the March 25, 1917,
Memorandum, to wit: that ships armed and under naval
orders to use that armament without restriction, and which
are also under orders to report enemy naval activity, can

be considered anything other than belligerently offensive

in nature.

[DIGEST OF INTERNATIONAL LAW, by Green Haywood Hackworth, Volume VI, Chapters XIX-XXI, Department of State, U. S. Government Printing Office, 1943, Pages 489-503.]

A Change of Face

On December 12, 1941, the Maritime Commission recommended to all operators of vessels of over 1000 gross tons operating on ocean, coastwise, or intercoastal routes, that their ships be painted immediately with nonreflecting "approved wartime grey;" and that those ships operating intercoastal and upon foreign trade routes have all exterior identification and distinguishing marks removed. Initially, the paint was supplied by the Navy.

[HISTORY OF THE ARMING OF MERCHANT SHIPS AND THE NAVAL ARMED GUARD SERVICE (an unpublished manuscript on microfilm) Division of Naval History, Department of Navy, Washington, DC]

The U-boatman's view of a merchantman as seen through a periscope was now quite indistinguishable from that of any naval or military auxiliary.

Writing during the post World War II years, Marjorie M. Whiteman, Assistant Legal Advisor to the Department of State, brought up the absurdity of expecting the enemy to make distinctions even if any distinctions had in fact existed between merchantmen and naval vessels. She relates that some merchantmen even performed the role normally carried out by naval fleet force ships. For instance, Whiteman cites Roskill's WAR AT SEA, 1954: Torpedo bombers making sorties against enemy ships flew off British aircraft carriers which were flying the Red Ensign of the British merchant marine. Other British merchant ships known as CAMs were equipped with catapaults for launching Royal Navy planes used in convoy defense actions. Dr. Whiteman, in a footnote on Page 675 of her work references the opinion of Tucker who dealt in depth with the subject in THE LAW OF WAR AND NEUTRALITY AT SEA, U. S. Naval War College, 1955.

"The 'common tendency of belligerents during World War II' to incorporate their merchant vessels into their military effort at sea has been responsibile, in Tucker's view, for the decline in 'importance of the earlier controversy over the effect of arming belligerent merchant vessels.'"

[DIGEST OF INTERNATIONAL LAW, Marjorie M. Whiteman, Volume 10, Department of State, U. S. Government Printing Office.]

PART III

NATIONALIZATION UNDER THE WAR SHIPPING ADMINSTRATION

FROM THE ENEMY'S VIEWPOINT: THE WAR AT SEA, 1939-1945

SUMMARY: U. S. MERCHANT MARINE IN WORLD WAR II

Unlike World War I, during World War II the nationalization of the United States oceangoing merchant marine was absolute as measured in the technical sense and close to absolute as measured by the mechanics of what actually occurred. Four months following the Japanese attack on Pearl Harbor, the United States Government at last made up its mind that in order to fight a global war, a total commitment of the nation's resources was required. For the merchant seamen dying unnecessarily off the east coast of the United States from German torpedoes because their ships' silhouettes were target outlined against the lights of coastal cities, this came as welcome news. By order of the Federal government made effective April 28, a nightly dimout was ordered for the Atlantic east coast for a width inland of fifteen miles. Earlier, on April 8, the War Production Board, by Executive Order had mandated that all construction (including ship and boatbuilding) not of a type essential to the war effort be stopped immediately.

On February 7, 1942, the War Shipping Administration (WSA) was created as an outgrowth of the U. S. Maritime Commission. WSA was to be the organization which would control and coordinate all U. S. merchant shipping, ie., allotment of new construction; recruitment

of merchant seamen; training of merchant seamen; and
allocation by assignment and b, charter of all existing
merchant ships. The allocation function of WSA was to
provide a pool of all oceangoing ships other than those
directly controlled by the Army or Navy. From that pool,
WSA would assign ships on a priority basis. In the
majority of cases, the Armed Forces was given priority;
however at times the lift of strategic materiels was
considered more important when viewed in the context of
the overall war effort.

Starting in April 1942, WSA put into effect the
war and emergency powers which had been granted the
President under the Merchant Marine Act of 1936
[Requisition or Purchase of Vessels in Time of Emergency:
Title 46 §1242 USCA.] Although no exact archival records
seem to be available, it is generally agreed by students
of the period that the entirety of the U. S. oceangoing
merchant marine had undergone requisitions by the latter
part of 1942. Under the plan, a number of methods were
used under which ships were assigned or allocated once
requisitioned:

** Following Governmental requisition, some ships
were bareboat or sub-bareboat chartered by WSA directly to

the military (Army or Navy) which then took over full operational responsibility including manning. If a vessel was badly damaged or lost under such a bareboat arrangement, then the operator (Army or Navy) took title to the ship, paying the owner (private shipping company or the Maritime Commission and later WSA itself) a certain price as predetermined at the time of charter.

** Under another method, those ships which were already owned by the Government (either the Maritime Commission or the old U. S. Shipping Board whose ownership was still extant) and which came from the Reserve Fleets were generally operated by the Government through a contractual arrangement known as Service Agreements made with either a general steamship agent or a shipping company acting as an agent. The agents then performed in a managerial capacity for an agreed-on fee. Under such a contract, the Master was recognized as the direct servant of the Government. Technically, under the Service Agreements, the master became the employer of the crew although in practice, the agent arranged for crewing and other services to the ship, all being carried out to the account of the Government. The seamen on such ships were considered the employees of the Government, although (following March 1943) they were not considered Civil Service nor were they included as employees of contractors with the United States under the provisions of Public Law 784 approved December 2, 1942. See Appendix A, this volume.

**   Under the terms of the charter agreement, the Government became the operator of ships requisitioned from their owners through a bareboat charter. Such ships were then management contracted either back to the owner or to another party which acted as agent on the same basis as in the previous example. The crews also were of the status as given in the previous paragraph. If a ship was lost, then her owners were compensated at a price which had been determined at the time of requisitioning.

**   This last arrangement provided that ships which had been requisitioned by the Government from their owners were time chartered back to the owners. The owners then operated them for a specified commercial purpose until such time that the WSA might require them for use elsewhere. It is believed that in the case of most company owned ships which were time chartered back to their owners, the manning and provisioning became the

responsibility of the owner. However, if the charterer
was not the vessel's owner, then WSA hired the crew by
Service Agreement. It is probable, though, that this
latter arrangement was not common since most who time
chartered under this arrangement were the vessel's
original owner. If the ship was lost, then her owner was
compensated at a price which had been determined at the
time of requisitioning.

Of the privately owned ships which were operating
under private control prior to April 1942, it is
practically certain that the only ones placed on a time
charter arrangement, as in the last example given above,
were those remaining in essential U. S. coastal or the
near foreign trades, these ships being mainly petroleum
tankers, colliers, and certain of the bauxite carriers.
Company owned ships which WSA wished to use on overseas
routes were almost always placed under bareboat charter
agreement to WSA, with the owning company acting as the
managing agent.

During the war years, all new construction was
for the Government. It is proper to presume that all dry
cargo vessels built between 1941 and 1945 were represented
within the first two requisitioning categories. Some of

the wartime tanker construction was undertaken to replace
the earlier wartime losses of the shipping companies.
Some replacement tonnage, at least that relevant to
companies engaged in the near foreign and coastal tanker
trade, may have been put on time charter arrangements
until assigned to transocean service.

Elmo Paul Hohman, writing while a Professor of
Economics at Northwestern University, gives an excellent
account of the WSA program in pointing out some
differences in ways by which the WSA dealt with its
operating agents. Hohman claims that when it came to
general labor practices, there was far less supervision by
WSA of time charter operators than was the case with
supervision of agents working under Service Agreements.
For instance, in the case of managing agents, any
discussions agreed upon between seamens unions and the
agent were not valid until endorsed by the War Shipping
Administration. As a result, after the first few months
of growing pains, the methodology of hiring, provisioning,
etc., on the part of the agents was standardized in all
ports. The time charter operator, on the other hand, was
relatively free to exercise his own labor relations,
methods of provisioning, maintenance, etc., provided, of
course, that everything was done in general conformity

with the standards established by the WSA sponsored
Maritime War Emergency Board and the overall War Labor
Board procedures.

[THE HISTORY OF AMERICAN MERCHANT SEAMEN by Elmo Paul
Hohman, Shoe String Press, Hamden, Connecticut, 1956,
Pages 85, 86, and 87]

The Service Agreement dealing with ships under
the control of WSA and entered into between WSA and its
management agents was a standardized document. Below is a
"Statement of Policy" issued in May of 1942 by the War
Shipping Administration. The reproduced document,
although referring specifically to crewing, is informative
regarding the general management of those ships
represented in the second and third requisition categories
I have earlier discussed.

May 4, 1942

"STATEMENT OF POLICY

"I. Existing Collective Bargaining Agreements to Stand.

"Article 3 (d) of the Service Agreement signed between Agents and the War Shipping Administration under which Agents handle vessels owned by or bareboat chartered to the War Shipping Administration shall remain in force and effect. This article reads as follows:

"'(d) The General Agent shall procure the Master of the vessels operated hereunder, subject to the approval of the United States. The Master shall be an agent and employee of the United States, and shall have and exercise full control, responsibility and authority with respect to the navigation and management of the vessel. The General Agent shall procure and make available to the Master for engagement by him the officers and men required by him to fill the complement of the vessel. Such officers and men shall be procured by the General Agent through the usual channels and in accordance with the customary practices of commercial operators and upon the terms and conditions prevailing in the particular service or services in which the vessels are to be operated from time to time. The officers and members of the crew shall be subject only to the orders of the Master. All such persons shall be paid in the customary manner with funds provided by the United States hereunder.'

"The intention of this clause is that in order to make available the full supply of officers and men and to avoid favoritism as to conditions between one agent and another, with respect to preference of employment or use of union hiring halls, all agents will be required to procure officers and men in accordance with such conditions."

[Vessel Crewing Files (Information File) Office Chief of Transportation Files, Modern Military Records Center, National Archives, Wash. DC.]

The overall intent of WSA in its process of taking over the merchant marine was to exert total wartime control while at the same time keeping intact the proven civilian mechanism by which the commercial shipping industry had historically been managed. Supplying and maintaining merchant shipping in peace is a highly specialized operation. It becomes far more complex under mobilization for total war. To have disrupted the workings of the proven mechanism through some form of temporary wartime apparatus, such as management by the U. S. Navy, would have been counter productive and far more costly to the war effort.

> Note: It should be said here that WSA was not "civilian" in the fullest sense since its top management was Naval in origin. For instance, Emory S. Land, Administrator, was a Rear Admiral, USN, on detached duty.

Certain aspects of the wartime expansion such as dealing with seamen recruitment and training, were, though, quite beyond the scope and experience of the peacetime industry. The WSA stepped in through direct participation regarding the developing need to care for seamen ashore and operation of overseas personnel replacement pools and other problems unrelated to peacetime shipping. The U. S. Maritime Service, a subsidiary operation of WSA, was by mid-war, operating training facilities on both coasts that were aimed at turning out entry grade officers; upgrading existing officers; and training thousands of "boot" seamen for unlicensed grade jobs.

The WSA maintained replacement seamen pools in the major theaters of war where it developed workable liason with the military and naval commands to which its ships were allocated. Once a ship was assigned a voyage, be it of military or civilian consignment, the actual routing and voyage control of the vessel was placed outside the purview of WSA, being entirely the responsibility of either the U. S. Navy or one of the navies of the British Commonwealth. This applied whether the ship was in convoy or sailing independently.

> Note: In practice, convoy discipline eminated from the Naval appointed "Convoy Commodore," usually a Naval officer who ordered the movement and conduct of the merchant ships in the convoy thus freeing the escort commander to fight off enemy attack. A ship traveling independently without inclusion within a convoy formation was under Naval orders to travel specific routes and abide by certain procedures and behavior while so routed.

Beyond a doubt, the War Shipping Administration successfully met the challenge of the wartime sealift while maintaining the industry within the framework of its prewar civilian management. This was also done by Britain which managed its wartime shipping through incorporating its Board of Trade into an Admiralty Section. When peace

came, for both the United States and Britain, the

transition from nationalization back to commercial control

was a smooth and orderly one.

> Note: For a comprehensive overview of the
> wartime WSA structure, I would suggest FEDERAL
> RECORDS OF WORLD WAR II, Volume I, Civilian
> Agencies, Gale Research Co., Detroit, 1982.

FROM THE ENEMY'S VIEWPOINT

THE WAR AT SEA 1939-1945

When World War II ended, the victorious Allies set up the Tribunals at Nuremberg at which the war criminals of Germany were to be tried before the world. The defendants were former military and civilian leaders within the Reich; their crimes were varied. One of the primary military figures to be accused was Grand Admiral Karl Doenitz, the architect of Germany's strategy for the submarine war against Allied shipping. Doenitz had a number of charges leveled against him, but only one is pertinent to this treatise, that being that he violated Article 22 of the London Protocols of 1930, Protocols to which Germany had been a signatory.

"THE LONDON NAVAL TREATY OF 1930
Article 22

"The following are accepted as established rules of International Law:
      "(1) In their action with regard to merchant ships, submarines must conform to the rules of International Law to which surface vessels are subject.
      "(2) In particular, except in the case of persistent refusal to stop on being duly summoned, or of active resistance to visit or search, a warship, whether surface vessel or submarine, may not sink or render incapable of navigation a merchant vessel without having first placed passengers, crew and ship's papers in a place

of safety. For this purpose the ship's boats are not regarded as a place of safety unless the safety of the passengers and crew is assured, in the existing sea and weather conditions, by the proximity of land, or the presence of another vessel which is in a position to take them on board.

"The High Contracting Parties invite all other Powers to express their assent to the above rules."

[U. S. STATUTES AT LARGE, Volume XLVI, Part 2, p. 2881-2882 (Wash.: U. S. Govt. Print. Off., 1931).]

The circumstances which led to the charge that Doenitz had broken the Protocol were a result of the primary reason why the Battle of the Atlantic (and its adjacent seas) was fought. The Atlantic battle, the longest and perhaps the bitterest of the war, was a contest for control of the sea lanes. Dominance over these supply routes would be the deciding factor of the war's outcome. From the German viewpoint, the targets of the Atlantic battle were Allied merchant ships upon which the survival of Britain depended as did the supply of Allied Armies, and the supply of strategic commodities which were fed into the factories of "Fortress America."

Up through 1942, the Battle of the Atlantic had been one of slugging attrition, Doenitz's basic strategy had been to sink merchant ships faster than the Allies, particularly the Americans, could build them; however by mid-1942, he realized that the war against ships was not in itself sufficient. He now ordered destruction of

ship's crews as well. It was this new order upon which
the prosecution at Nuremberg drafted the specification
against Karl Doenitz. As it turned out, the charges would
result in the placement of a question of guilt upon both
the Axis and Allied navies.

The first certain evidence of the Doenitz order
came to light in the summer of 1944 following the capture
by British forces of the U-852. Its commander,
Kapitanleutnant Heinz Eck, was tried by a British military
court martial for atrocities committed during Eck's
sinking of a Greek freighter the previous March. During
the trial, Eck testified that prior to leaving port in
occupied France, his submarine flotilla commander Kapitan
Karl Moehle briefed him that: 7

> "Rescue runs counter to the most elementary
> demands of warfare for the destruction of enemy ships and
> crews."

Moehle, later put under interrogation at the
Nuremberg Trials explained those 1942 instructions. He
made the statement that it had been clear to anyone
familiar with the manner in which his superior Admiral
Doenitz issued orders,

> "...that the High Commander regarded as desirable that not
> only ships but also their crews should be regarded as
> objects of attack, that is, that they should be
> destroyed. At that time, German propaganda was
> continually stressing the shortage of crews for enemy
> merchant ships and the consequent difficulty. I, too,
> understood the order in that way."

During the earlier court martial of Eck, a witness for the defendant, one Leutnant Peter Heisig, stated that in late 1942 when Admiral Doenitz addressed a graduating officer class of midshipmen, he told the novice officers -- Heisig was one of them -- that the Allies were launching over a million tons of shipping a month which was more than the German U-boats could possibly destroy. Therefore, from "now on," U-boatmen should carry on total warfare against ships and crews.

Embarrassingly for the Allies, Doenitz's trial brought to light that British and American submariners--individually and as a matter of command policy--had also violated the London Protocol of 1930 as they too had directed all out warfare against Axis merchant ships. The sad facts are that merchant seamen, both Allied and Axis, had universally been targeted to die. 8 Fortunately for Allied seamen, the ever-improving Allied anti-submarine warfare efforts restricted U-boats from surfacing, so deck gun fire directed at torpedoed ships trying to get-away their boats was not as frequent as it might have been. At times, humane attitudes continued to be exhibited by some German U-boat commanders; however, the occasional acts of offering water, rations, and other kindnesses which a few U-boatmen

had extended early in the War soon became a thing of the
past. 9

Mallison discusses the charge against Doenitz and
the specification against Article (22) of the London
Protocol of 1930. He disputes the specification's
charge's realism, arguing that it was doubtful whether
there were a significant number of merchant ships which
were not actively participating in the war and/or were not
in the status of having become hostile units. Mallison
maintains that the rescue provision under the Protocol did
not apply to those ships which had lost their innocent
merchant ship status through participating in the war.
[Mallison, Page 135]

"Shortly after the outbreak of War, the British
Admiralty...armed its merchant ships, in many cases
convoyed them with armed escorts, gave orders to send
position reports upon sighting submarines, thus
integrating merchant vessels into the warning network of
naval intelligence. On 1 October 1939, the British
Admiralty announced that British merchant ships had been
ordered to ram U-boats if possible."

[Nuremberg trial transcript as paraphrased within U. S.
Naval War College, INTERNATIONAL LAW DOCUMENTS, 1946-47
(1948), Page 299.]

In evaluating the program of Allied integration
of its merchant vessels into the network of naval
intelligence, Mallison further argues that such
integration taken by itself placed those vessels well
outside of the status of being merchant ships and

therefore on that basis alone, Germany's unrestricted

attacks against ships and crews was justified.

Burdick Brittin wrote in 1981:

"Civilians lose their immunity from deliberate
attack when they take direct part in hostiliites. Whereas
members of the armed forces may be attacked whether they
are engaged in combat or not, civilians are subject to
deliberate attack only 'for such time' as they take a
direct part in hostilities. Clearly, civilians who try to
kill, injure, or capture enemy persons or damage enemy
material are taking a direct part in hostilities. The
same would be true of a civilian who was acting as a
member of a weapons crew. A civilian providing
intelligence information to combat units, such as an
artillery spotter or member of a ground observer corps,
would also be subject to attack while he was carrying out
that function. On the other hand, civilians providing
indirect support to the armed forces, such as workers in
defense plants, would not be subject to deliberate,
individual attack, although they might have assumed the
risk of incidental injury as a result of attacks on their
places of work."

"... A person's behavior, location, and
appearance will all be relevant factors in deciding
whether or not he is a civilian."

[INTERNATIONAL LAW FOR SEAGOING OFFICERS, 4th Edition, by
Dr. Burdick H. Brittin, Naval Institute Press, 1981, Pages
220-22 and Pages 248-50.

Note: In addition to being an author on the
subject of the law of the sea, Brittin served as
the Director of the International Law Division of
the Navy's Judge Advocate General's Office.

Doenitz was acquitted on the specific charge of
having violated Article 22 of the London Protocol. He was
convicted and later sentenced to prison on the separate
charge of waging aggressive war.

Note: Much of the Nuremberg debate involving Article 22 revolved around the British action in initially arming its merchantmen in 1939-40. The testimony, therefore, tended to predominantly describe the British experience. It must be remembered, though, that American policy duplicated the British example upon U.S. entry into the war in 1941.

Allied Policy Toward Axis Merchant Ships

The treatment of our merchant shipping by the enemy was almost exactly parallel to our treatment of theirs. Mallison is especially aware of this.

"The Japanese merchant ships like the British were armed, reported submarine sightings and attempted to ram or otherwise attack submarines. In short, such merchant ships were functionally incorporated into the Japanese naval force. Consequently, there can be no doubt but that these merchant ships were the lawful objects of 'unrestricted submarine warfare,' that is, attack without warning within the operational area enforced by submarines. These are the principal reasons for the conclusion of the legality of the United States submarine operational area in the Pacific." [Mallision, Pages 89, 90]

A press release issued by the U. S. Navy in early 1946 provides perhaps the best synopsis of the Pacific war as it was conducted against merchant ships. It effectively summarizes the tragedy that befell the thousands of civilian seamen of both sides who died in that Pacific conflict.

"The conditions under which Japan employed her so-called merchant shipping was such that it became impossible to distinguish between 'merchant ships' and Japanese Army and Navy Auxiliaires."

[Press Release, "U. S. Submarine Contributions to Victory in the Pacific (14) Feb 1, 1946, Navy Department as referenced by Mallison, his Page 122.]

Our Navy claimed, and with justification, that it could not distinguish the enemy's "merchant ships" from its "military auxiliaries." It seems that all sides were faced with the same problem; all ships not only looked alike, but they acted alike.

The result of the unrestricted sea war is well portrayed by the statistics of United States WW II merchant ship losses through enemy action. All together, the U. S. lost 527 merchant ships. As a point of comparison, the U. S. Navy combat loss for all classes of commissioned vessels, including its small craft, totaled 455 vessels, 72 fewer than the U.S. merchant ship losses.

> Note: The United States Army lost 40 of its military auxiliaries in the categories of large troopships, dry cargo ships, and tankers. The Army's small craft losses have not been accurately tallied as of this writing.

[BRITISH AND FOREIGN MERCHANT VESSELS LOST OR DAMAGED BY ENEMY ACTION DURING SECOND WORLD WAR, 3 September 1939 to 2 September 1945, BR 1337, Naval Staff (Trade Division), British Admiralty (American Vessels Lost by Enemy Action) Revision of AFO 105/50]

[UNITED STATES NAVAL VESSELS LOST DURING THE WAR (WW II), Navy Department Publication, 2 October 1945]

SUMMARY

U. S. MERCHANT MARINE IN WORLD WAR II

Nationalization

Prior to April of 1942, that entity known as the American Merchant Marine was a composite of publicly and privately owned shipping, all of its ships being engaged by private operators within trade and commerce for the purpose of creating profit. In April 1942, a government agency known as the War Shipping Administration (WSA), through authority of Executive Order, as granted under the war and emergency powers, began nationalizing U. S. shipping. By late 1942, virtually all oceangoing and coastwise shipping had been brought under WSA control. The greater part -- probably all of those ships assigned to transocean routes -- was being operated by WSA through service contracts executed between the Government and shipping agents (or shipping companies which acted as agents.) The remainder shipping, primarily coastal tankers and colliers, was, upon its requisitioning by the government, subsequently time chartered back to private shipping companies, those time charters being subject to immediate cancellation at the pleasure of the Government whenever the ships were needed in other service.

The War Shipping Administration, in a study prepared in 1946 entitled THE UNITED STATES MERCHANT MARINE AT WAR, claimed that during the four years of war, WSA allocated up to 75% of its controlled tonnage to Army and Navy cargoes. It is probably accurate to say that few, if any, ships were not allocated to direct military use at some point during their wartime career. A corresponding claim could be made for the wartime assignment record of the individual seaman.

According to the WSA report, the 25% of shipping tonnage that was not concurrently allocated to military use was utilized

"...in the lend lease program; civilian exports needed by Allied nations; and programs established by the State Department and Foreign Economic Aid Administration for shipments to Latin America and other countries; and imports of strategic materials for war industries and essentials for civilian use."

# # # # #

Trade and commerce had effectively ceased. Merchant ship bottoms were, without exception, dedicated to the strategic goals of the United States war effort.

Militarization

Appearance. During December of 1941, operators of merchant ships were ordered by the Maritime Commission to remove all identifying marks and to paint ship hulls and superstructures in "approved Navy grey." After that, there was no way to distinguish, vis-a-vis appearance, a merchant ship from a military or naval auxiliary.

Armament. All oceangoing and coastal merchant ships were armed as soon as guns became available. Following early 1942, all "defensive fire only" restrictions were lifted; thereafter, orders to merchant crews and Naval Armed Guards were "fire on sight." Masters were ordered to "ram."

Gunnery Assignments. Naval instructions as issued by the Chief of Naval Operations in 1940 (before merchant ships were armed) instructed merchant marine masters to coordinate with Naval Armed Guard commanders in the assignment of members of the merchant crew to supplement the Armed Guard. This became effective when the first Naval armament went aboard a merchant ship on December 1, 1941. The instructions were augmented by specific orders of the War Shipping Administration, issued on January 25, 1943, that all merchant ship masters were to order their crewmembers to gunnery stations on a specific assignment basis. This meant that on the typical cargo ship or tanker, the entire crew -- less those actually engaged in maneuvering the vessel -- was assigned to gunnery duties.

Intelligence. Merchant ships were integrated into the Naval intelligence network. This occurred even prior to our entry into the war, but was not a mandated program until after the Declaration of War, December 7, 1941.

Military Discipline

Throughout the entire war, military discipline under the Articles of War (Army) encompassed those merchant seamen who were on ships engaged in the carriage of military cargo or personnel.

Merchant seamen, whenever in overseas areas which were under U. S. military control, were subject to all of the Articles of War (Army) including Article 15. (This was the Article under which Martial Law and the Provost Court system was put into force.)

Following December 31, 1942, the high seas and military occupied overseas areas were considered by the Navy Department to be "zones of military operations;" and therefore, following December 31, 1942, merchant seamen in ocean service were placed under Naval control and

discipline. A merchant seaman assigned by a ship's master
to a battle station under the control of a Naval gunnery
officer subsequently came under the direct command and
discipline of that officer. (A Naval Courts and Boards
ruling in 1937 had declared that merchant seamen came
under Naval control and discipline whenever within an area
deemed to be a "zone of military operations.") See
Appendix B for a more thorough discussion of the
discipline factor.

# # # # #

AMERICAN MERCHANT SEAMEN WHO SERVED IN OCEANGOING SERVICE
DURING WORLD WAR II PERFORMED THEIR DUTIES UNDER A LEGAL
FRAMEWORK WHICH, IN LIGHT OF ALL RECOGNIZED INTERNATIONAL
LAW, PLACED THEM INTO THE ROLE OF COMBATANTS INTEGRATED
WITHIN THE ARMED FORCES OF THE UNITED STATES.

COMMENTARY NOTES

1 Safford, now a Professor of Economics at Montana State University, also authored WILSONIAN DIPLOMACY, 1913-1921.

2 The deKerchove definition for "Auxiliary Vessel" then continues on, discussing the term as it would also apply to "fleet train," or fleet auxiliary -- those being vessels which are considered a part of the commissioned naval force and which normally accompany a naval fleet, ie., naval fleet tankers, naval ammunition ships, etc..
        There is yet another meaning for which the term "auxiliary" is used, but only when prefixed with "combat" as in "combat auxiliary." An example of this use was within the Naval Limitation Agreements as reached in Washington in November 1921. There the term was applied to destroyers and light cruisers in auxiliary service to capital ships. [Morison, page xxxvi.]

3 The functions of the World War I civilian agencies, ie., the U. S. "Shipping Board" and the U. S. "Fleet Corporation" and "operating agents" thereto, were closely duplicated during World War II by the the U. S. Maritime Commission and its outgrowth arm, the War Shipping Administration which appointed operating agents working under Service Agreements. For an excellent organizational description of the World War I U.S. Shipping Board and the U.S. Fleet Corporation, the reader is referred to Pages 80 through 83 of the document MIXED CLAIMS COMMISSION, UNITED STATES AND GERMANY - ADMINISTRATIVE DECISIONS AND OPINIONS OF A GENERAL NATURE AND OPINIONS Government Printing Office, Washington, DC 1925.

4 The two commission members and the Umpire were in complete agreement over twelve of the cases. A dissenting vote was cast by the American Commissioner on the issue of the thirteenth, the USAT JOSEPH CUDAHY. The dissention was made on the basis that USAT JOSEPH CUDAHY was in ballast (having previously unloaded her cargo) at

the time of loss. The original opinion was upheld and
thus carried into effect by the two-third "majority"
consisting of the German Commissioner and (American)
Umpire Parker, they reasoned:
"The fact that she was in ballast at the time of
her destruction is immaterial. Being a tank ship
operated by and for the exclusive use of the Army
Transport Service of the United States, her
return in ballast for additional supplies of
gasoline and naptha for the United States Army on
the fighting front was an inseparable part of her
military operations."
[Mixed Claims Commission, JOSEPH CUDAHY Opinion, Case
No. 547.]

5   During   World   War   II,   military   and   naval
auxiliaries were utilized by volume and in diversification
of types in greater quantity than had previously been
known. For instance, the United States Army, on 1 August
1945, had under its absolute control 186 large ships each
in excess of 1000 gross tons. Additional to this, the
Army had a sizeable fleet of manned small craft (under
1000 tons and/or under 200 feet. The large ships were
manned with Civil Service crews; the smaller units carried
civilian and/or military crews in various combinations. A
few   of   the   crews   were   mixed   civilian/military   with
civilian officers and Army enlisted men for crewmen;
however this last was not the normal situation.
[Transportation Corps (3 vols), U. S. ARMY IN
WORLD WAR II, The Technical Services, Office of the Chief
of Military History, Department of the Army.]
The enemy also made extensive use of auxiliary
vessels. In the case of the Japanese, that use did not
stop with surface craft. In order to supply their widely
scattered garrisons, the Japanese had a small fleet of
supply submarines which were manned by soldiers. [U. S.
Strategic   Bombing   Survey   (Pacific)   Naval   Analysis
Division, Interrogation of Japanese Officials - Submarine
Warfare, OPNAV-P-03-100, Nav No. 72, USSBS No. 366, 10 Oct
1945.]

6   Unfortunately,   some   distortion   has   been
introduced into the historical files. Comments made by a
reserve officer on active duty for training in the postwar
years, while he was undertaking a review of some World War
II Armed Guard reports, were addended to the archival
study, ARMING OF MERCHANT SHIPS AND THE NAVAL ARMED
GUARD. The comments infer that the generalized "problems"

between merchant marine crews and Naval gun crew
detachments were the exclusive fault of the merchant
crews. Monitoring of the reserve officer's work brought
criticism (also within the file) from his superior who
felt the reservist's report lacked sufficient citation of
evidence for such a charge.

Viewing it from another aspect, Jordan Meilach in
his book BELL BOTTOM SHORTS writes informally of his
actual experience aboard merchant ships while an enlisted
member of the Naval Armed Guard, serving with three
separate Armed Guard detachments. He tells of a Naval
Armed Guard Commander under whom he served who spent most
of his time harranging the Navy gunners and signalmen as
to what "low lives" the merchant crewmen were. Meilach
claims to have once openly corrected that officer by
accusing him of being not only a bigot but a totally
incorrect one as well. Meilach relates that the same
Armed Guard officer "froze" during an air raid when the
ship was in North Africa; Meilach claims that the merchant
master was consequently forced to direct the gunnery
personnel during the remainder of that action. In
appraising the relationship, as he saw it, between
merchant crews and the Armed Guard, Meilach wrote,

"During my three year duty among several merchant
ships, I know of only two individuals [merchant
seamen] that strayed from the straight and
narrow. I only wish the Navy had such a record."
[BELL BOTTOM SHORTS, Carlton Press, 1968, New York, Pages
54-57 and 69.]

Court records document one "problem": That
incident started with a drinking bout attended by merchant
and Naval personnel while a ship was in a South American
port. It ended with the death of a ship's officer who was
attempting to restore order. That officer was shot to
death by machine gun fire which had been turned on him by
one of the drunkards, a member of the Naval Armed Guard.
[Reinhold v/ U. S. (2 CCA) 1948, AMC, 921 167 Fed 556].

The "problems" were, in most cases, brought about
by a small number of malcontents within both the merchant
marine force and the Armed Guard. In the case of the
merchant marine, these were people who found shipboard
employment and sometimes retained it only because of the
acute shortage of the overall wartime labor force. In the
case of the Armed Guard, there was sometimes a tendency
for the Navy to "get rid" of people who were considered to
be disciplinary problems by assigning them to the Armed
Guard rather than the fleet force.

On most ships, the majority of the merchant seaman and naval gunners behaved well; they lived, fought, and sometimes died together as compatable shipmates serving together in a common cause.

7 Kapitanleutnant Eck had been commander of the German submarine U-852. On the night of 13-14 March 1944, while in the South Atlantic, he torpedoed the Greek merchant ship PELEUS. Panicked that the resultant floating debris would disclose the proximity of his position to any patrolling Allied aircraft, he cruised his U-boat through the survivors, sinking by machine gun fire and grenade most everything including most of the crew of the PELEUS. A handful of crewmembers escaped detection by hiding under rafts. When they were later rescued, they reported on what had happened. Some weeks later, while in the Indian Ocean, U-852 was itself attacked and damaged. Eck beached the U-boat on the African coast where, by a strange quirk of fate, he and his crew were captured by the British controlled Somaliland Camel Corps. Eck was convicted of the atrocities he committed against the PELEUS crew and was executed by a firing squad.

8 Testimony for the defense of Admiral Doenitz was offered by Kapitan Bernhard Rogge who had commanded the ATLANTIS, a German surface raider sunk by HMS DEVONSHIRE in November of 1941. Rogge testified that the British had made no attempt to rescue the ATLANTIS crew or the crew from an accompanying supply ship, the PYTHON, which was sunk at the same time. In all, 414 Germans were left to the sharks. Fortunately German U-boats which had picked up Rogge's distress call arrived in time to rescue most of the survivors.
    Another case of British atrocity committe against a ship's crew was also brought out. The ALTMARK, a German supply ship was captured by the British in Norwegian waters in February of 1940. The gunners of the capturing British destroyer fired at the German sailors who attempted to flee across the ice. A similar instance also took place in Norwegian waters when the Royal Navy sank the German minesweeper ULM on 14 September 1942. German survivors in the water were machine gunned. The British justified their action by the statement:
    "The usages of war permit shooting at crews to
    prevent their reaching shore and rejoining the
    enemy's fighting force."

[TRIAL OF THE MAJOR WAR CRIMINALS BEFORE THE INTERNATIONAL MILITARY TRIBUNAL, NUREMBERG, 14 November 1945 to 10 October 1946, Vol XL, Nuremberg, 1947-49, Doenitz - 39, pp. 61-65, as referenced in Footnotes to Chapter 10 of THE TRIALS OF THE GERMANS by Eugene Davidson]

It is noted that in the case of ULM and ATLANTIS the crews were German Navy. In the case of ALTMARK and PYTHON, the crews were merchant seamen serving on auxiliary ships.

From the onset, the United States Navy practiced a war of attrition against the Japanese merchant marine, and that warfare was, by policy and by practice, conducted against Japanese merchant seamen as well. "Quarter" was not a consideration.

9 To help set the record straight, it is proper here to point out differentiations between the practices of the Germans and the Japanese. In a number of instances, Japanese submariners, with a flair bordering on pleasure, actually executed the survivors of sunken merchant ships. Merchant marine personnel who are known to have suffered under such treatment were from the following Allied ships: SS DAISY MOLLER in December 1943, SS BRITISH CHIVALRY in February 1944; SS TJISALAK in March 1944; SS RICHARD HOVEY in March 1944; SS JEAN NICOLET in July 1944. There may have been others. In the case of the above ships, there were a few survivors who lived to tell the tale. What happened aboard other ships from which there were no survivors, but which are known to have been sunk by the Japanese is, of course, a question without answer.

PART IV

APPENDICES

APPENDIX A

THE TREATMENT OF MERCHANT SEAMEN AND CIVIL SERVICE SEAMEN

REGARDING THEIR ...

MAINTENANCE AND CURE; DISABILITY AND DEATH BENEFITS

WORLD WAR II

In dealing with this subject, it is necessary to approach the matter of benefits from two separate standpoints: The first is the situation with merchant seamen. The second is the situation regarding civilians employed under Civil Service by a military arm of the Government, ie., U. S. Army Transport Service (later U. S. Army Transportation Corps., Water Division.)

MERCHANT SEAMEN

Death and Disability Benefits

Merchant seamen are not ordinarily covered by forms of employee compensation benefits. In lieu of that, the seaman has the privilege of recovery for damages under general maritime law whereby if he is injured in the service of his vessel (other than as a result of his own misconduct), he has limited rights for wages, maintenance, and cure. He collects wages for the time he cannot work, commencing with the beginning date of his disability, until either the voyage terminates or until he recovers, whichever occurs first. Maintenance and cure continues until he recovers or further cure is considered unavailing.

Beyond this, the vessel can be held liable for damages on account of loss of life or injury if the vessel is found "unseaworthy" (or) if the vessel can be found negligent as is enabled under the Jones Act [October 1920, Sec 33; 41 Stat 1007]. Under the latter, the contributory negligence of the seaman does not bar claims, but it may reduce the amount of recovery. As the years have gone by, increasing liberalism over favoring the seaman's position under the Jones Act is evident in case law when compared against the years preceeding World War II. When damages are caused through the fault of another party--say, another ship -- then if that ship is found fully negligent in collision with one's own vessel, it would be thus held liable for personal injury or death caused to persons on the held harmless vessel.

"Prior to 1942 when the government took over the merchant marine, [a] privately employed seaman had not only his remedy under this section [Title 46 §688, USCA] but also his rights under the general maritime law enforceable in admiralty or by various forms of proceedings elsewhere. Hust v. Moore-McCormack Lines, Or.1946, 66 S.Ct. 1218, 328 U.S. 707, 90 L.Ed. 1534."

The outbreak in hostilities and the subsequent takeover of the merchant marine by the Government in 1942 created problems not handled by the above methods. Damages caused by a belligerent force were obviously uncollectable unless provided for through some form of post-war mechanism, such as the Mixed Claims Commission, which was established following World War I under the provisions of the Treaty of Berlin. To take care of the situation which arose with World War II, the United States Maritime Commission met with representatives of shipping companies and licensed officer groups during August 1941 and agreed on a War Risk Insurance plan of $5,000 for an individual seaman's policy to cover loss of life. Unlicensed seamen were not covered. The policies were made part of the employment benefits with no premiums due

on the part of the officers. The National Mediation Board
extended this to cover government operated (Maritime
Commission) ships as of November 10.

On December 18, 1941, President Roosevelt
established the Maritime War Emergency Board, a joint
endeavor of the Maritime Commission and the Department of
Labor with advisors appointed from the shipping industry
and from various maritime unions. One of the earliest
decisions of that Board was their establishment of War
Risk Insurance as applicable to all segments of the
merchant marine (both Government and private) and
retroactive to December 7, 1941. The insurance was also
extended to cover unlicensed men. By successive
amendments, coverage was changed to embrace certain other
war risks not directly attributable to injury received by
a seaman while serving aboard his own particular ship;
these included death and disability while a prisoner or
while being repatriated. Later, with a revision to the
War Risk Insurance policy, certain marine casualties were
also brought in "by umbrella"--at least in those cases
where exigencies of war were considered to have
contributed to the damages. This last inclusion took
place on April 23, 1943, as a result of the discretionary
powers allowed under Public Law 17, which had been signed

into law in March.   The amount of the policy remained at

$5,000, only half of the insurance then allowed under life

benefits to members of the Armed Forces.   The Maritime War

Emergency Board, through the War Shipping Administration,

repeatedly tried to have Congress raise the amount to

$10,000, as experience had already shown that the policy

benefits which were intended to cover cases of permanent

disability, could be exhausted after a relatively short

period of time.   Under existing legislation no other

method could be found by the Board to assist such

disability cases or their families.   Neither the doctrine

of "Maintenance and Cure," or suits for damages through

the courts were claimable liabilities against the vessel

in cases of established war risk.

[HISTORY OF THE MARITIME WAR EMERGENCY BOARD, (a monograph
report) prepared for the United States Department of Labor
by Francis B. Goertner, Washington 1950, Page 119.]

According to Goertner, the Board believed

"...that it was practically impossible to distinguish
between the bulk of cases in which the elements of wartime
operations might have claimed to be absent."

In analyzing the general actions of the Maritime War

Emergency Board, it seems that the Board felt a primary

responsibility toward the taxpayer; therefore, it often

"drew the line and knowingly [some] people were not taken

care of."   [Goertner]   That   quotation   pertained

particularly to those who, because of wartime stress, suffered medical and psychological breakdown; these people were usually left out of war risk coverage and could not claim through any other existing avenue.

Under Public Law 449, which was approved on September 30, 1944, an amendment was added to Public Law 17 (referred to in the statutes as 57 Stat 45). This allowed the War Shipping Administration to extend disability payments to permanently disabled seamen beyond the extent of the $5,000 war risk policy, once that amount had been expended, and to do so in accordance with the same rate schedule as would be applicable under what was then and now known as the Federal Employees Compensation Act (FECA). Thus, for the time being at least, seamen who were killed or permanently disabled while in line of duty, were covered through an ongoing monthly payment program, extending beyond the $5,000 insurance. That added relief was short-lived.

On June 23, 1947, the Senate Committee on the Judiciary, writing in Senate Report No. 339, WAR AND EMERGENCY POWERS - TERMINATION, declared that the parent legislation for War Risk Insurance, ie., Subtitle - Insurance, Title II of Merchant Marine Act, 1936 (added by Act of 1940) was applicable only for six months after the war, a date since past. That Act was thereby "Repealed" by resolution, the [Senate] committee having been informed that such action, "is in accord with the views of the Maritime Commission." Presumably, those who expected their monthly disability check, as either principals or heirs, were abruptly cut off. Legislative attempts (H.R. 2346 filed June 20, 1946) to bring these disabled persons permanently under the purview of the Federal Employees Compensation Act failed. The country's willingness to recompense seamen who, because of wounds, were disabled in service, or survivors of merchant seamen who had been killed, had abruptly ceased as of June 1947.

Another pension provision (referenced in the main body of this treatise) was allowed under §225 of Title 46. As described in the United States Code Annotated, it provides for pension payments for war deaths or wounds -- but only for licensed officers. Its language provides that those serving during war in the capacity of "merchant marine officers in the service of the United States" are entitled to all the privileges accorded to soldiers and sailors serving in the Army or Navy." My own investigation through conversations with the Claims Division of the Veterans Administration has disclosed no evidence of application being made under this Act by

officers (or by heirs of officers) who either served with
the War Shipping Adminstration or who served aboard
vessels owned or operated by the War Department. This is
not to say that forty years ago persons did not apply to
their local V.A. offices only to be turned away for some
reason known only to the local bureaucrat. A record of
such an application would never have reached the
Washington Claims Division files.

> Note: I am informed that following my disclosure
> of the existence of this law, Congress is
> investigating (February, 1986) why the Act was
> never utilized.

As the history of the early war years tell us,
starting in April of 1942, the War Shipping Administration
began to rapidly nationalize the merchant marine under the
war emergency powers which authorized the Government to
requisition privately owned bottoms. Once requisitioned,
such ships legally became "public vessels." 1 Their
masters and crews subsequently became officers and
employees of the War Shipping Administration and
therefore, by implication, employees of the United
States. Technically crews, at least at that time,
automatically came under FECA. It is not known whether
claims were ever filed by WSA seamen under FECA during
that period. If they were filed, it cannot now be
ascertained whether or not they were ever processed.

This automatic eligibility under FECA must have caused concern to those in the Government when thinking of the potential postwar costs. This was probably the reason why on March 24, 1943, within the prelude of Public Law 17, the Congress proclaimed:

March 24, 1943 [H.R. 133]
[Public Law 17]

"Be it enacted by the Senate and House of Representatives of the United States of America in Congress assembled, That (a) officers and members of crews (hereinafter referred to as 'seamen') employed on United States or foreign flag vessels as employees of the United States through the War Shipping Administration shall, with respect to (1) laws administered by the Public Health Service and the Social Security Act, as amended by subsection 9b) (2) and (3) of this section; (2) death, injuries, illness, maintenance and cure, loss of effects, detention, or repatriation, or claims arising therefrom not covered by the foregoing clause (1); and (3) collection of wages and bonuses and making of allotments, have all of the rights, benefits, exemptions, privileges, and liabilities, under law applicable to citizens of the United States employed as seamen on privately owned and operated American vessels. Such seamen, because of the temporary wartime character of their employment by the War Shipping Administration, shall not be considered as officers or employees of the United States for the purposes of the United States Employees Compensation Act, as amended; the Civil Service Retirement Act, as amended; the Act of Congress approved March 7, 1942 (Public Law 490, Seventy-seventh Congress); or the Act entitled 'An Act to provide benefits for the injury, disability, death, or detention of employees of contractors with the United States and certain other persons or reimbursement therefor,' approved December 2, 1942 (Public Law 784, Seventy-seventh Congress). Claims arising under clause (1) hereof shall be enforced in the same manner as such claims would be enforced if the seaman were employed on a privately owned and operated American vessel..."

It is clear, then, that the only thing granted
merchant seamen which gave relief for war risk deaths,
wounds, or injuries was the miserly $5,000 War Risk
Insurance policy, as extended September 30, 1944. 2 In
June of 1947, the Congress retracted that extension.

Medical Benefits

Medical care for war wounds and other ship board
injuries was given under the standard privileges granted
seamen through the Public Health Service Marine
Hospitals. This care continued for those who were in need
of ongoing treatment and medical custody. It was a
somewhat different matter for those who later developed
secondary conditions. Those men ran up against a 60-day
rule which, under Public Health Service Regulations,
required that a seaman applicant for medical aid had to
have been employed as a seaman within 60 days from the
date of making application for hospitalization or
out-patient care. In the early 1980s, the Public Health
Service ceased providing medical aid to merchant seamen
through the Marine Hospitals; consequently, the men who
since the war had been receiving continuity of care were
turned out. It has been stated to me by the Council's

Office of the Public Health Service that most, if not all, of those men were placed under other forms of hospitalization, either through federal or local programs, both public or charitable in nature. However, since statistical records on the disposition of such persons are not extant, the latter statement is based on hearsay only.

Veterans Benefits?

At the time of the passage of the G. I. Bill of Rights, President Roosevelt, on June 22, 1944, stated:

" I TRUST THAT THE CONGRESS WILL ALSO PROVIDE SIMILAR OPPORTUNITIES FOR POSTWAR EDUCATION AND UNEMPLOYMENT INSURANCE TO THE MEMBERS OF THE MERCHANT MARINE, WHO HAVE RISKED THEIR LIVES TIME AND TIME AGAIN DURING THIS WAR FOR THE WELFARE OF THEIR COUNTRY."

Congress did not react as Roosevelt had asked. Five Bills were considered in Congress during the mid-1940s. Additional efforts to have Bills introduced were made following the war but without success. Had these Bills succeeded, then at least those disabled who did not possess skills commensurate with employment for the disabled could have retrained through educational provisions such as those provided through the G. I. Bill.

The reasons behind the opposition to this

legislation cannot, at this late date, be thoroughly
analyzed; however, antagonism against the Bills appears to
have stemmed from the following:

a)   Organized lobbying, particularly from the
        American Legion and the Veterans of Foreign Wars.

b)   A supposed inequity in pay between merchant
        seamen and members of the Armed Forces. This has been
        exposed as fallacy. In October of 1945, Hearings
were conducted before the committee on the Merchant Marine
and Fisheries, House of Representatives. The subject of
the Hearings was "Benefits to Merchant Seamen." Due to
strong opposition by existing veteran's lobbies as well as
a strong anti-union sentiment at the time running through
the Congress, two bills, H.R. 2346 and H.R. 3500 never got
out of Committee. During the Hearings, a letter addressed
to the National Commander of the American Legion and
written by Telfair Knight, Assistant Deputy Administrator
for the War Shipping Administration, was introduced as
evidence (Pages 101, 102, and 103 of the Hearing
transcript). In the letter, Mr. Knight presented a
detailed analysis of the comparison in pay between members
of the Armed Forces and the merchant marine. This letter
is here reproduced:

War Shipping Administration,
Training Organization,
Washington 25, D.C.

Mr. Arren H. Atherton,
    National Commander, the American Legion,
       National Headquarters, Indianapolis, Ind.

Dear Mr. Atherton: This will acknowledge receipt of your letter of October 27, 1943, in which you stated the position of the American Legion with regard to inclusion of Merchant Marine seamen on Legion honor rolls. If these community honor rolls are dedicated specifically to "those serving in the armed forces," then of course merchant seamen are not technically eligible. If, however, any are dedicated to "those in the war service," "in the service of our country," or "of the United States," then it is believed proper that merchant seamen should be included. We cannot of course agree that service in the merchant marine can be, in any way, considered as only equivalent to home guard, civilian defense, etc., since these activities have few casualties directly attributable to enemy action, as has the merchant marine. The casualty lists show that the percentage of casualty in the merchant marine is at least three or four times the percentage for any of the armed forces.

We wish further to correct an impression which you have in regard to the pay of men in the merchant marine. We believe it particularly unfair to compare the highest paid merchant seamen to the lowest-paid member of the armed forces, as is done so often. Particularly, you mention that the gun crew on board merchant vessels draw from $50 to $80 per month. For your information, all Navy personnel assigned to Navy gun crews are at least seamen first class. The base pay for this rate is $66, with a 20-percent sea-pay bonus, bringing this to $79.20, which is the very smallest pay drawn by any member of the Armed Guard. The ratings for other members of the Armed Guard range up to petty officer second class, the base pay plus allowances for that grade being $115. The above, of course, is minimum and applicable only to single men without dependents. If he is married or has dependents to whom he allots $22 per month from his pay, the Government pays to his dependents further allowances in accordance with the following table:

Wife... $50
Wife and child ($20 additional each child).. 80
Child, no wife ($20 additional each child).. 42
Divorced wife only (not exceeding amount provided by court order).................. 42
Divorced wife and child ($2- additional each child)............................... 72
1 parent (chief support).. 50
2 parents (chief support) ($11 for each additional brother or sister)............ 68
1 parent and 1 brother or sister ($11 for each additional brother or sister)...... 68
Brother or sister, no parent ($11 for each additional brother or sister).......... 42

It can thus be seen that a married man with two children serving in the armed guard will be paid from $157.20 to $193.20, depending on his rating.

This compares with a base pay of $72, which, with 15 percent special emergency raise, is $82.50 for ordinary seaman (who have had a least 3 months in training at $50 per month, comparable to the length of training for the seaman first class of the armed guard), plus a bonus ranging from 40 percent to 100 percent. For able seamen the base pay is $82.50 with a 15-percent special emergency raise, bringing it to $100. The merchant seaman, therefore, gets as his total base pay an amount varying between $115.50 and $200 per month. Overtime pay averages about 30 percent of base. No allowances are granted for dependents. Every man serving aboard a merchant vessel, with the possible exception of the master and chief engineer, could earn more money ashore in a shipyard or defense plant without taking the chance of being killed by bombs or torpedoes.

You also mentioned that the Navy gun crew cannot quit their ships. This is, of course, true; but it is also true that in return they are paid for 12 months per year, with 30 days' leave allowed per year, with pay. They are also paid during periods of transfer and stand-by. The merchant seaman is paid only for such time as he is serving aboard ship and has no leave with pay, except in a few isolated istances. He can, however, take a specified maximum leave between voyages without pay. A merchant seaman's pay starts only after signing on a ship and stops as soon as the ship is paid off in its home port. He is paid for an average of 10 months per year, while the Navy man is paid for 12 months per year. From actual pay rolls of ships on various runs, the War Shipping Adminitration has determined that the average monthly pay for ordinary seamen is $197.50; and for able seaman, $231.25. All this is subject to income tax. This includes wages, voyage bonuses, and overtime. The following table shows a comparison of average gross income received by four men, each with a wife and two minor children. Two are Navy men paid for 12 months, and two are merchant seamen paid for 10 months:

Comparison of gross income of merchant seamen with Navy enlisted men after deduction of income taxes

	Navy sea-man, first class	Navy petty officer second class	Ordinary Seaman	Able Seaman
Monthly Pay (wife and 2 children)	$157.20	$193.20	$197.50	$231.25
Yearly pay (12 months for Navy; 10 months, merchant seamen)	1,886.40	2,318.40	1,975.00	2,312.50
Less exclusion of pay for military personnel	1,500.00	1,500.00	------	------
Estimated gross income	386.40	818.40	1,975.00	2,312.50
Less:				
Personnel exemption (wife and 2 children)	1,900.00	1,900.00	1,900.00	1,900.00
Estimated surtax net income	------	------	75.00	412.50
Less earned income credit	188.60	231.81	197.50	231.25
Estimated normal tax net income	0	0	0	181.25
Victory tax:				
Estimated Victory tax net income	386.40	818.40	1,975.00	2,312.50
Less exemption	624.00	624.00	624.00	624.00
Balance subject to tax	0	194.40	1,351.00	1,688.50
Summary:				
Estimated surtax (13 percent)	------	------	9.75	53.63
Estimated normal tax (6 percent)	------	------	------	10.87
Estimated Victory tax (5 percent)	------	9.72	67.55	115.62
Tax	------	9.72	77.30	180.22
Gross income	1,886.40	2,318.40	1,975.00	2,312.50
Tax	------	9.72	77.30	180.22
Income after tax	1,886.40	2,308.68	1,897.70	2,132.28

It will be noted that the ordinary seaman and seaman first class compare favorably, as do the petty officer second class and the able seaman.

There are some other major differences on the question of compensation which are not direct pay but still are definite factors. A merchant seaman who is totally and permanently disabled will be paid benefits at the rate of $200 per month until the disability has ceased or until a total of $5,000 is paid, whichever first occurs. Where the disability has been established so that it will continue to remain permanent, an additional benefit of $100 per month is paid to the insured until a total of $2,500 more is paid. Payment then stops, with no further extension of benefits. The cash value of such insurance, which provides for only 75 monthly payments of $100 to one who is totally or permanently disabled, is $6,290. A members of the Armed Guard who is a petty officer third class (median grade for Armed Guard) who is physicaly incapacitated and medically surveyed will receive a payment of $58.50 per month for so long as he lives. At the age of 25 the cash value of such an annuity is approximately $11,500. It will be noted above that the merchant seamen must be totally and permanently disabled, while the Navy man needs only to be physically incapacitated and can supplement his pension by working at a civilian job, which cannot be done by a merchant seaman who is totally and permanently disabled.

To the dependents of merchant seamen killed goes a flat sum of $5,000. To the dependents of a Navy man killed goes the base pay for 6 months. This, for the petty officer third class, would be $468. However, his dependents would be eligible for pensions for the rest of their lives on a varying scale but, roughly, as follows: Wife, $50; first child, $20; second and additional children, $10 each.

The wife would draw this pension for life or until she remarried. The children would draw the pension until their eighteenth birthday.

If a man leaves a wife, age 25 (life expectancy, 44.73 years), she would receive if she remained unmarried, $50 per month for 45 years, or the sum of $27,000. Taking remarriages into consideration, the average widow would receive a total of $15,350. If he leaves, in addition, two children, 5 and 3 years of age, they would receive totals of $3,120 and $1,800. The amount of money to purchase an annuity based on the above averages would be $15,300, which could be called insurance.

In addition, the Navy seaman has the privilege of purchasing additional national service life insurance up to an amount of $10,000 for a premium of less than $1 per month per $1,000. This low-priced insurance he may continue to carry even after leaving the service. A merchant seaman is permitted to purchase additional insurance up to an amount of $15,000, for which a premium of $2 per month per $1,000 is charged. However this insurance is on a month-to-month basis and cannot be continued while the seaman is ashore. The insurance applies only while on the vessel. If a merchant seaman is hit by a truck while ashore, he receives no compensation for being incapacitated, even though injuries received makes him totally incapacitated. A Navy man's insurance is applicable in such a case.

In addition to all the above very material differences, there are many other benefits accruing to naval personnel which have a definite monetary value. Some of these are free medical attention for the dependents of Navy seamen and the privilege of hospitalization of dependents at the very nominal rate of $3,75 per day for any cause

This includes all medical attention, medicine, and other expenses. Confinement cases for wives of petty officers third class and below are free of charge. A Navy man below chief petty officer receives an initial issue of approximately $133 worth of clothing. Every quarter after the first year he receives an allowance of $8.75 for clothing. The merchant seaman pays for his own. The Navy man who elects to make a career of the Navy is also eligible for pension upon his retirement after a specified number of years of service. There is no provision by which merchant seamen can serve any number of years or be eligible for any pension. Free postage, the reduced furlough rates for travel, reductions on theater tickets, and on meals while traveling and other privileges are benefits which in time do total an appreciable amount.

We realize that this is a rather lengthy letter, but we also feel sure that in all fairness you will appreciate being advised of the facts. The commonly accepted opinion that merchant seamen are too well paid is thus seen to be a myth, and it would be appreciated if the American Legion could help to dispel this myth by advising all its posts of the true facts in the case. The men who are merchant seamen are men from the same towns and homes as the men in the Army and Navy. Their services to their Nation are important, and we feel sure you will agree now that the facts are known that they are not overpaid. Many are sons of members of the American Legion, and many are veterans of the last war. I myself am a member of the American Legion and know that the Legion is interested in fair play and justice.

Your cooperation is dispelling the misconception in regard to merchant seaman's pay will be greatly appreciated.

Very truly yours,

Telfair Knight
Assistant Deputy Administrator for Training

c)   <u>Also not to be overlooked and I think of</u>
        <u>paramount importance, was that at the end of the war,</u>
        <u>beginning in 1946, the maritime unions repetitiously</u>
        <u>struck for wage increases.</u> These frequent strikes
called by the union leadership were the result of a
competitive race for supremacy within the overall union
movement. The seamen themselves suffered most from this
contest which played its part in the virtual destruction
of the American Merchant Marine as a major force in world
shipping. Often (because of the then open balloting on
strike issues) the seamen had no realistic say over what
was happening to their industry. The strikes were often
punctuated with violence on the part of union "goon
squads." Accordingly, any legislation favoring a group
whose image had become tarnished by this labor militancy
was doomed to failure. The heroes of the Battle of the
Atlantic were thus forgotten by a Congress that now began
viewing them as a group threatening the postwar economic
recovery.

        It is ironic to look back upon this when you realize
that the vast majority of the men who sailed the ships in
wartime service had but limited involvement in these
postwar strikes. Most of the WW II seamen had returned to
the mainstream of American life by the time the strikes
began. 3

CIVIL SERVICE SEAMEN

Unlike merchant seamen, Civil Service seamen who saw service aboard vessels owned and/or operated by the War Department, received some pension benefits through the medium of their Government employment. As Civil Service employees, (both permanent and temporary) these men came under both the Civil Service Retirement Act and the Federal Employees Compensation Act.

Federal Employees Compensation Act

Under the Federal Employees Compensation Act, (FECA) a seaman who had been wounded from enemy action or who suffered from injury received in line of duty which resulted in a permanent disability, was entitled to permanent disability payments. (Heirs of those killed received pensions as well.) Payments under FECA differed considerably from those payments which have been paid over the years to disabled Armed Forces veterans (or their heirs). FECA payments are based upon capacity to earn; while veterans' disability pensions remain constant despite any changed earning capacity of the recipient. Both FECA pensions and veterans' pensions under the administration of the Veterans Administration have been incrementally increased over the years to allow for rises in cost of living.

War Risk Insurance and Pay Generally

The War Department generally paid its seamen upon the same wage scale as that used to pay merchant seamen under standards as established by the War Shipping Administration (WSA). The patterning after the WSA system was a mechanism by which the Army could remain competitive in attracting seagoing personnel. The policy for this was spelled out in War Department Memorandum W620-40-42 dated October 31, 1942, entitled WAR DEPARTMENT POLICY GOVERNING VESSELS OPERATED BY THE WAR DEPARTMENT. To effectively implement the program of pay equality, it was soon realized that an informal liason would have to be established between the Army and the Maritime War Emergency Board. Channels of communication were opened during March 1943, and one of the first items of agenda was the War Risk Insurance program. War Risk Insurance ($5,000) had earlier been made available to Army seamen by the War Department, but now, by inter-agency agreement, it would be handled to the account of the Army by WSA's insurance department. Payments made to a seaman (or his heirs) were offset against any payments made under the Federal Employees Compensation Act; therefore, for most Army seamen, the War Risk Insurance benefits as a practical matter, became a relatively moot issue. Despite that, the existence of the War Risk Insurance program probably helped recruitment as many seamen might have felt prejudiced against (in comparison with WSA employment) had the insurance benefit not been in existence.

On the matter of bonuses, the Army promligated its own system. For its larger vessels, bonus categories, like wages, were developed along lines almost identical to those of the War Shipping Administration. However, the system for contract personnel serving on the Army's smaller ships in overseas theaters, as well as for certain of the large ships on permanent overseas theater assignments, differed quite extensively from the WSA pattern. Under the Army's contract system, overtime could be negated by order of the Theater Commander. Needless to say, those orders became standard operating procedure, and overtime pay for those serving under such contracts was virtually eliminated. [Contract Form: WD-TC-CPD #2 SWP.

(A similar form was used in the ETO.)] Unlike the merchant seamen, Army seamen, were granted earned sick leave and annual leave with pay under the Civil Service system.

Following the war, Army seamen, like their merchant marine counterparts, did not receive any additional benefits through federal legislation.

HISTORY OF THE WAR EMERGENCY BOARD, Appendix II, (unpublished), contains a complete discussion of wage and bonus practices for Civil Service seamen as carried out by the War Department, 1941 - 1945.

* * * * *

COMMENTARY NOTES: APPENDIX A

1 Those vessels owned by or under demise charter to the Maritime Commission were subject to the U. S. Navigation Laws and pertinant regulations; however as the term applied to other U. S. statutes, the ships are still "public vessels."

2 The reader is again reminded that within the statutes (§225, Title 46, USCA) there existed the provision -- seemingly never applied under -- that merchant marine officers serving in their licensed capacity while in the service of the United States, if wounded or killed, are eligible for the same pension benefits as administered for members of the Army and Navy. Unlike other statutes dealing with veterans benefits, this provision is obscurely tucked away in the Shipping Section of the U. S. statutes; it has never been codified within Title 38, USCA, which deals with Veterans Benefits. Consequently, persons who might have qualified under this provision were not made aware of its existence. This author stumbled across it by accident while researching Title 46 on an unrelated matter.

3 It was a bitter irony to members of the U. S. merchant marine, WW II, that Congress later passed into law the authorization for the Veterans Administration, "to provide hospitalization, outpatient, and domiciliary care to certain former members of the armed forces of the Government of Czechoslovakia or Poland who participated during World War I and II in armed conflict against an enemy of the United States and who have been citizens of the United States for at least 10 years." [Public Law 94-491]

APPENDIX B

DISCIPLINE

MERCHANT SEAMEN - CIVIL SERVICE SEAMEN

Merchant Seamen

Shipping - Title 46 §701, Offenses and Punishments

This law applies to merchant seamen "lawfully engaged, or any apprentice to the sea service." [§701 Title 46, USCA]

"Merchant Seaman in this title [Title 46] simply means seamen in private vessels as distinguished from seamen in the Navy or public vessels, and seamen employed on private vessels of all nations are 'merchant seamen' and literally included in this phrase: U.S. v Sullivan, C.C. Or.1890, 43 F602. See also Scharrenberg v Dollar SS Company, Cal 1917, 38 S.Ct.28, 245 US 122, 62 L.Ed. 189." [Title 46, §713, Note 15, USCA]

Under Title 46, Officers (excluding masters) are generally considered seamen.

"A third officer is a 'seaman' as defined in this section, relating to merchant seamen, and is generally regarded as a seaman, and will be treated as a ward of the admiralty as in the case of an ordinary and able seaman. Ames v American Export Lines, D.C. NY 1941, 41 F. Supp 930." [Title 46 §713, Note 16, USCA]

Under §701, eight offenses are specified. The
first five deal with those wherein the ship's master can
impose his direct discipline. The latitude allowed a
master here is considerably broader than that which can be
imposed directly by a unit commander in either the Army or
Navy. For instance, in the case of the Army, deprivation
of rations, confinement in irons or forfeiture of pay was
expressly forbidden under Article of War 104 (unit
punishment of a non-judicial nature). 1   In the Navy,
"Captains Mast" allowed more latitude than did the Army's
Article of War 104.

The offenses (and disciplines) discussed under
§701, Title 46, USCA, which allow the master to directly
punish an offending seaman:

"(1) For desertion: forfeiture of effects and of wages
earned. 2

"(2) For neglecting to join up or absence without leave:
forfeiture of two days' pay.

"(3) For quitting the vessel after arrival in port before
she is secured: forfeiture of not more than one month's
pay.

'(4) For willful disobedience of any lawful command at
sea: to be placed in irons until the disobedience ceases,
to lose not more than four days' pay (or, at the
discretion of the court, imprisonment for not more than
one month).

'(5) For continued disobedience or neglect of duty at sea:
to be placed in irons on bread and water with full rations
every fifth day until such disobedience shall cease, by
forfeiture of twelve days' pay for every twenty-four hours

of disobedience or neglect (or by imprisonment of not more than three months at the discretion of the court)."

The remaining specifics which are given below all dealt with those sentences which could only be imposed by a Federal court to which the master delivered the offending seaman:

6) Assault of master or mate: not more than two years' imprisonment.

7) Damaging or embezzling from vessel: not more than one year's imprisonment.

8) Smuggling: not more than one year's imprisonment..

Criminal Code of the United States

For other crimes at sea, the merchant seaman was subject to the same charges and punishments permissable under the Federal Criminal Code as applicable to any other civilian or member of the military. Inherent to his command function, the master of a ship has the police power to take any measure of restraint which may be required in order to safely bring the offender before a federal court of justice. The police power of the master, in such cases, extends to all aboard, including passengers, both civilian and military. During the war, the master was empowered to ask the assistance of any military forces aboard his ship, either for the purpose of apprehending or assisting in the confinement of offenders.

Disciplinary Authority of U. S. Coast Guard

Contrary to popular impression, the Coast Guard's disciplinary authority over merchant seamen was limited during the war (and still is) to its control over the occupational certificating and licensing of the individual seaman. Such is not to imply that this control is of a minor nature. On the contrary, it is extremely important to the individual since any suspension or revocation of a certificate or license bars the person so penalized from employment on U. S. merchant vessels.

Prior to World War II, the authority for suspension or revocation of seamen's documents was vested in a civilian agency known as the Bureau of Marine Inspection and Navigation an agency within the Department of Commerce. On February 28, 1942, the functions of that Bureau were transferred by Executive Order to the Coast Guard. 3   The Coast Guard by then had become a part of the U. S. Navy, having itself been earlier transferred from the Treasury Department to the Navy. Militarization of the entity that controlled seamen's certification and licensing was initially viewed with alarm by the seamen's unions which thought of it as the beginning of a military takeover of their industry. Prior to Coast Guard takeover, most of the actions against certificates and licenses had resulted from offenses dealing only with charges of the most flagrant insubordination or derelictions of duty, this being particularly so in the case of unlicensed personnel. With the sudden expansion of the merchant marine and the necessity to take on men who in peacetime might not otherwise have been employed,, troublemakers of various varieties found their way into the sea service. According to Reisenberg, writing in SEA WAR, part of the reason for this was that the Selective Service system did not begin granting draft deferments to merchant seamen until May of 1942. Prior to that time, experienced seamen were taken off ships and entered into the Army; "draft culls" who had never been to sea consequently found shipboard employment in their place. These untrained people who did not have a background of disciplinary control were, it appears, the seamen who caused most of the early problems. An attempt to deal with this was a primary reason for transferring the old civilian Bureau of Marine Inspection and Navigation to the Coast Guard. The War Shipping Administration gradually weeded out these troublemakers ("performers" as the unions termed them) by recommending that the Coast Guard remove their seamen's certificates. The shipping companies and maritime unions cooperated in this endeavor.

[Executive Order, Redistribution of Maritime Functions, #9083, effective February 28, 1942] [SEA WAR by Felix Reisenberg, Jr., Reinhart and Company, Inc., 1956, Pages 98-99] [Memorandum to Asst. Sect. of the Navy Bard, 13 July 1943 signed R. R. Waesche, Vice Admiral, USCG]

Military Discipline as Generally Applied

In peacetime, once a merchant seaman steps off his vessel, he is no longer subject to the control of the ship's officers. The only deviation from this can occur in those cases where a serious shipboard crime had been committed; in such cases, the master could request that civil authorities apprehend the offenders. In overseas ports, the U. S. Consular Service could be called upon by the Master to enforce shipboard discipline.

When the war started, it was obvious that the inability to effect discipline against seamen ashore while in theaters of active military operations or to impose direct military control when required in cases where ships were allocated to a military or naval mission could become handicaps to efficient military operations.

Prior to World War II, the Army's position as to its authority over merchant seamen through the vehicle of military law is given in Judge Advocate General Opinions. These were derived from the experience of World War I and

before. The Army had considered civilians "accompanying
or serving with the armies of the United States in the
field,   both   within   and   without   the   territorial
jurisdiction of the United States" as being subject to
military law in time of war.   [Article of War 2]   Colonel
Lee S. Tillotson in his THE ARTICLES OF WAR - ANNOTATED,
The Military Service Publishing Company, Harrisburg, PA,
1942, (pages 8-9), claims that prior to the First World
War military jurisdiction was rarely applied to civilians
except to those who were serving "in a quasi military
capacity with troops in a theater of war, such as
teamsters, watchmen, employees of the supply department,
telegraphers,   interpreters,   guides,   contract   surgeons,
railroad and transport employees, etc."   Apparently, those
who provided periphery type support to the military but
who were not actually attached to any Army organizations,
were free of prosecution under the Articles of War.
Enforcement in the cases of "quasi military" categories
was limited by what the Army then considered "in the
field."

     With the onset of World War I, Tillotson tells us
that   jurisdictional   interpretation   broadened   to   a
geographical identification which included those employed,
"along the lines of communication who were, 'serving with

the armies in the field,' and at Ports of Embarkation

which were 'a part of the lines of communication.'"

Civilian employees at ports, within the United States

territorial limits were thus included as subject to

military law. Colonel Tillotson then goes on to say that

the words, "in the field do not refer to land only but to
any place, land or water, apart from permanent posts or
fortifications where military operations are being
conducted. The following classes of persons have been
held subject to military law under this Article [Article
2]: civilian employees on mine planters and transports;
all persons on board Army transports, either passenger or
freight or on any vessel operating under the jurisdiction
of the War Department for purposes connected with the
operations of the Army;..."

The last category, "persons... on any vessel operating

under the jurisdiction of the War Department" has been

construed as applying to any merchant vessel operating

under a time charter or allocation to the use of the Army

while used in support of the Army's operations, even

though the crew might not be employed directly by the Army.

"A merchant ship which was part of a large convoy
transporting military supplies to Africa through submarine
-infested waters was 'in the field' within provision of
former section 1473(d) of this title subjecting to former
Articles of War persons accompanying Armies of United
States in the field, so as to subject to court-martial a
merchant seaman on such ship for violation of former
Articles of War while on high seas." [Note 70, Title 10
§802, USCA.]
        "A military voyage for the purpose of
transporting army troops and supplies during war is a
military expedition 'in the field' within cl. (10) of this
section relating to persons subject to military law.
McCune v. Kilpatrick, D.C. Va. 1943, 53 F.Supp. 80."

In October of 1942, the War Department addressed commanders of theaters, Ports of Embarkation, etc., that military control could be exercised over merchant seamen but preferred that when civilian tribunals were present that they should handle all but the most severe matters. The first reference I have found to a policy of rigid enforcement of military discipline appears in a United States Naval Fleet (European Theater) communication of June 8, 1943. Although the communication is of Naval origin, it references the jurisdiction of the Army over merchant seamen in specific situations. The entirety of that June 8, 1943, communication is reproduced below:

```
                         "UNITED STATES FLEET
              UNITED STATES NAVAL FORCES IN EUROPE
Please refer             20 GROSVENOR SQUARE
to file: A17              LONDON, W.1.
```

Serial 1186   June 2, 1943

From: The Commander, U.S. Naval Forces in Europe
To: The U.S. Naval Liaison Officer, Liverpool.
      The U.S. Naval Liaison Officer, Belfast.
      The U.S. Naval Liaison Officer, The Clyde, Gourock.
      The U.S. Naval Liaison Officer, Bristol Channel Area,
          Cardiff, Wales.

Subject: Disciplinary   jurisdiction   to   be   exercised   over
          merchant   seamen   in   the   European   Theatre   of
          Operations; agreement relative to.

     1.   Respecting the above subject, the following understandings
have been reached between Headquarters, European Theatre of
Operations, U.S. Army, and this Headquarters:
          (a) U.S. Navy vessels are regarded as being exclusively
               under the jurisdiction of the Navy;

          (b) U.S. Army transports are regarded as being exclusively
               under the jurisdiction of the Army;

          (c) The U.S. Navy will be responsible for administering
               the discipline of merchant seamen aboard U. S.
               merchant vessels:
               (1) While enroute to and/or from this theatre of
               operations; and
               (2) After arriving and/or while in an United Kingdom
               port; EXCEPT

          (d) The U.S. Army will be responsible, during unloading
               and loading for turn-around, for administering the
               discipline of merchant seamen serving aboard vessels
               allocated to the War Department by the U.S. War
               Shipping Administration, and turned over to the Army
               at the port of destination;
```
```

(e)   The U.S. Navy will be responsible for administering the discipline of merchant seamen while ashore — except in those cases which the Navy and Army authorities decide shall be turned over to the Army for trial and punishment. Implementing the discharge of this responsibility of the Navy, the military authorities will turn over to the Naval Port Authorities merchant seamen arrested by military authorities in the vicinity of the port;

(f)   In administering merchant seamen discipline the existing disciplinary machinery of the U.S. War Shipping Administration and U.S. Consular Service will be utilized as far as possible consistent with naval and military responsibilities for securing and aiding the war effort.

2.   While such jurisdiction is to be exercised whenever the exigencies of military operations so demand, it is especially important that all officers charged with the administration of this responsibility be ever mindful that the primary object of its exercise is to facilitiate the accomplishment of the miltary effort being served by such seamen. Accordingly, appropriate instructions will be issued to your subordinates and steps taken to see that this authority is exercised with tact and in a manner which will not hamper the War shipping Administration in its service to this theatre.

/s/ H.R. STARK"

Generally speaking, in putting this disciplinary policy into force, it seems that if the offense occurred on shipboard and the master could cope with it, then he handled it. If it was beyond his control, he called in the military. However, when the offense, either ashore or aboard ship, was of a nature to hamper the conduct of the vessel's military mission, then it became a matter for the Army or the Navy. One court decision helps bring this into focus:

> "Where jurisdiction of military commission over merchant seaman must be found solely in the law of war because of inapplicability of former section 1473 of this title or Articles for Government of the Navy, section 1200 of former Title 34, Navy, or a declaration of martial law, jurisdiction hinges upon a determination of whether acts of seaman were to the detriment of the success of the United States military operations. Hammond v. Squier, D.C. Wash. 1943, 51 F.Supp. 227." [Note 72, Title 10, §802 USCA]

> "Merchant seaman, whose act in striking civilian superior aboard merchant vessel containing military cargo in foreign port in active theater of military operations was not to the detriment of success of United States military operations, was entitled to be dealt with under the section governing offenses and punishments under the law of shipping. Hammond v Squier, D.C. Wash. 1943, 51 F.Supp. 227. [Note 36, Title 46, §701 USCA]

In jurisdictions such as the British Isles, where the civil justice system was adequate, and provided the local civil authority asked for jurisdiction over a civil offense, then the use of that local country's system, in consultation with the United States Consular Service, usually was put into play. Generally, most shore offenses committed in Europe involving routine disorders became a problem for the Navy; however, when many of the ports on the Continent came into use following the Invasion of Normandy, these ports came under the exclusive jurisdiction of Army with no Naval authority present. Shore offenses committed by merchant seamen in those areas were thus handled by the Army. It is probable that in the Pacific, jurisdiction over merchant seamen was flexible, depending solely upon who was conducting operations in the particular area. In the Southwest Pacific, which was MacArthur's domain, jurisdiction came under the Army; elsewhere, if the Navy had control, then the Navy would have had jurisdiction over any merchant seamen who were on the scene. Military justice in overseas areas where the Army was in control was usually implemented through Provost Courts established under the martial law authority of Article of War 15.

The basis under which any judicial authority, whether civilian, Army, or Navy, was imposed upon a merchant seaman was effected upon the seaman's inclusion under Shipping Articles. Until an individual had affixed his signature upon Shipping Articles, he was not identifiable as a merchant seaman under any point of law.

Attachment to a ship through Shipping Articles was the vehicle which gave him his merchant marine status. Entry upon Shipping Articles was undertaken in the presence of a Shipping Commissioner while in the United States, or if overseas, then before a U. S. Consul. The authority that a U.S. Consul possessed in that regard was emphasized in Navy Department Regulations §1.165:

"<u>Merchant Crews</u>.
        "Vessels under the jurisdiction of the Navy in foreign ports having merchant crews are amenable to navigation laws. Crews must be shipped and discharged before consuls and papers posted with consuls, except in those cases where anticipated orders for prompt movement makes this course undesirable in which case the consul is to be notified.
        "The regulations of the Department of State concerning merchant vessels and seamen, see 22 CFR, Parts 81-88, 22 CFR Cum. Supp., Parts 116, 117 [circa 1943]."

[Cumulative Supplement to the Code of Federal Regulations of the United States of America, Title 33 in Title 45; Title 34--Navy, Chapter I--Department of the Navy; Divison of the Federal Register, U. S. Government Printing Office, Washington, 1944.]

Navy Operational Discipline And Control Over Merchant Seamen

As mentioned elsewhere within the main text, the Navy, through a ruling of Naval Courts and Boards in 1937, §333, had stated:

"The officers, members of crews, and passengers on board merchant ships of the United States, although not in the naval service of the United States, are, under the laws of the United States, the decisions of the courts, and, by the very necessities of the case, subject to military control while in the actual theater of war."

It was this 1937 Courts and Boards ruling that set the stage for the wartime Naval disciplinary control which was to follow. Because of disciplinary problems reported to have occurred aboard some merchant ships, Rear Admiral Emory S. Land, Administrator of the War Shipping Administration, addressed a memorandum (October 8, 1942) to all agents of WSA for transmittal to ship's personnel. This was a prelude to what would follow from Naval authorities.

WAR SHIPPING ADMINISTRATION

Washington

October 8, 1942

TO ALL GENERAL AGENTS AND AGENTS OF
VESSELS OWNED BY OR CHARTERED TO THE
WAR SHIPPING ADMINISTRATION

The War Shipping Administration is concerned that slack
discipline aboard ship, both at sea and in foreign ports, continues
in the present war situation. Lack of discipline and order aboard
ship, particularly when military operations are affected, cannot be
allowed to continue.

To this end you are advised that:

1. When vessels are part of an active task force or are
    operating in theatres of war, the Masters are subject to
    the order of the commanding Officers of the appropriate
    force or theatre, and disobedience on the part of the
    Master and crew to such orders may subject the Master and
    crew to military discipline.

2. When vessels are not part of an active task force or are
    not operating in theatres of war, the control and authority
    over the vessel rests solely with the Master, subject to
    the directions of the War Shipping Administration.

3. When vessels are on the high seas whether in convoy or
    operating alone, the Master must, at all times, follow the
    routings prescribed for the convoy or the vessel by United
    States Naval authorities, and disobedience on the part of
    the Master to such orders may subject the Master to
    military discipline.

4. Organizations of licensed and unlicensed personnel are
    being supplied with copies of this letter.

                              (Sgd.) E. S. LAND
                                     E. S. Land
                                     Administrator

On December 25, 1942, a "Restricted" message signed by Commander in Chief of Naval Operations, Ernest J. King, was sent to all Naval units. Paragraph 4) of that message read:

"4. Serious offenses by masters and crews of merchant vessels, in the theater of war, which jeopardizes the safety of the ship or cargo or tend to impede the prosecution of the war should be treated in accordance with Chapter IV, Section 333, Naval Courts and Boards. In connection with the subject of this paragraph refer to my confidential dispatch 031240 of October 1942."

[FF1/A14-1, Serial 6077, 25 Dec. 1942 (Copy of this message is contained within Naval Department Bulletin, Cumulative Edition, published December 31, 1943, Dept. of Navy Library, Wash. DC)]

On December 31, 1942, the Navy declared its full intentions with a communique addressed to all merchant marine interests ashore and afloat:

"All waters, outside the territorial waters of neutral and unoccupied countries, have been declared to be a zone of military operations.

"Cases of lack of discipline or refusal by crew members to obey the orders of the master should be immediately reported to Naval Task Force or Task Group Commanders, or other Naval authority in all cases where military operations or the efficient conduct of the vessel concerned may be prejudiced.

"Naval officers have been directed to exercise the authority mentioned above whenever military consideration requires. Any person who refuses to obey the orders of a Naval officer in the exercise of this authority is punishable by an Exceptional Military Court or by Federal Civil Authority.

"This memorandum should be brought to the attention of the officers and crew of all merchant vessels with the admonition that Naval officers will not hesitate to exercise the powers conferred on them whenever a report is received of an actual or threatened breach of discipline by civilian personnel."

Signed J. W. GREENSLADE

District Staff Headquarters, Twelfth Naval District, Dec.
1, 1942 (P 13-9; 34073-14-B/Sk. W. Greenslade. Copies
sent to all Pacific Naval Commands; Convoy Commodores;
USA; Ship Operating Agents; Naval Advocate Gen Center
Pacific, et al.]

Essentially, this order gave the Navy its first
opportunity to prosecute errant seamen under the naval
court system. It also established a direct authority
which Armed Guard commanders could exercise over merchant
seamen whenever the latter were at gunnery stations to
which they had been assigned by the ship's master. (It
did not, however, usurp the overall authority of a ship's
master, either over his own crew or over the Armed Guard.)

It is presumed (reference last line, second to
last paragraph of the Greenslade letter) that the Navy
also had absorbed the prosecution power given a Consular
Officer under Title 46, USCA §685 and §703 through acting
as the party bringing charges at a Federal Court of
Jurisdiction in the United States. However the use of
military law no doubt would have remained the most
appropriate avenue of prosecution for an offense committed
overseas.

Summarization:

Military and Naval Discipline Over Merchant Seamen:

Prior to December 31, 1942, the disciplinary rein
on merchant seamen by the military was only spasmodically
applied, at least in the sense that the location and
employment of the ship they were on determined the
bringing to bear of that discipline. With the new Naval
policy inaugerated in December 1942, this policy had
changed to one of more routine enforcement where and
whenever the military thought it to be necessary to impose
its control. Military control began once a ship left a
United States port and was at sea and it extended to any
foreign place which possessed the presence of an Allied
military or naval force. Essentially, the only place
where a merchant seaman could now count on being
completely free of military discipline once ashore was in
the continental United States and a few U.S. territories
such as Hawaii, Puerto Rico, or the Virgin Islands.

Discipline and control by military and naval
authority could be direct or it could be through the
surrogate form of the ship's master. Backup for the
latter could be called upon from a military or naval force
ashore or afloat or it could be more immediate in the form

of assistance from the Naval Armed Guard.

On February 19, 1945, the Adjutant General of the Army, in a lengthy document, layed out specific and detailed standards for applying military discipline. These were contained in War Department Pamphlet No. 27-5 entitled MILITARY JURISDICTION OVER MERCHANT SEAMEN. Page 2 of the pamphlet, Paragraph 6, proclaimed, 'that military tribunals have jurisdiction not only over Army Transports, <u>but also over the crews of vessels, American and foreign, which are within a base or military area, or are carrying cargo (materiel or personnel) in connection with the military or naval operations of the United States in war.</u>"

Despite its introductory reference to the Gerlach case (Gerlach was a crewman on an Army transport), Pamphlet No. 27-5 was not a guide for the disciplinary administration of Army seamen. Rather it was addressed solely to the handling of merchant marine personnel under military law as well as procedures to be followed vis a vis the United States Consular system which was applicable only to merchant marine personnel.

Civil Service Seamen on Auxiliary Vessels of the Army

Disciplinary authority exercised by the military over Civil Service seamen differed in many respects from military authority exercised over merchant seamen. The differences are sometimes confusing to those unfamiliar with maritime law. Even such an able historian as the Army's Wardlow has exhibited some misunderstanding of the distinctions. Those misunderstandings revolve mainly around the applicability of Title 46, USCA.

The sections of Title 46 of the U. S. Code Annotated covering "Offenses and Punishments, within §701, §702, §703, §706, §707, §712, §713 only applies to merchant seamen. It does not apply to seamen serving on "public vessels" owned by the military and/or operated by the military through bareboat or sub-bareboat charters.

"Merchant Seaman in this title [Title 46] simply means seamen in private vessels as distinguished from seamen in the Navy or public vessels, and seamen employed on private vessels of all nations are 'merchant seamen' and literally included in this phrase: U.S. v Sullivan, C.C. Or.1890, 43 F602. See also Scharrenberg v Dollar SS Company, Cal 1917, 38 S.Ct.28, 245 US 122, 62 L.Ed. 189.' [Title 46, §713, Note 15, USCA]

Authority over crewmembers aboard auxiliaries is brought about through their contractual obligation (be it from entry on ship's articles or other contract form) to the Government, whereupon they bring themselves under the regulations of the military service. The same punishments as outlined in §701 paragraphs (1), (2), (3), (4), (5) were designated by the Army under its Regulations as applying to its Civil Service seamen; however, the authority of the master to impose those punishments was under the Army's own Regulations -- not under the statutes within Title 46.

The Army's use of ship's articles under which some of its marine personnel were employed was actually an extension of the seaman's Civil Service obligation. It was a method to contractually bind an employee to a particular ship for a stated term or voyage. Without such a contractual obligation, the seaman, in the same fashion as most other categories of civil servants, would have been free to resign at will. 4 The Army, however, did not always use the article form of contract. In the case of civilian seamen who were sent overseas for employment on small craft or as crewmembers to serve on the larger vessels which were permanently stationed in theaters of operation, a one year contract was executed. These contracts were generally unspecific, naming the starting place of employment and thence "to any place in the world." On other types, a specific theater of operations might be named, ie., "Southwest Pacific."

Certain civilian graduates of the Army's small ship officers' schools were bound to employment for the duration of the war plus six months. 5

Whether bound by articles or by contracts, enforcement of employment terms as well as general discipline control was the sole purview of the Army. The civilian jurisdiction as exercised over merchant seamen did not apply.

"A consular officer of the United States has no jurisdiction whatsoever over the members of the crew of Army chartered [meaning bareboat chartered] transports or tugs, either when a member is under arrest or under confinement by direction of the master, or when in service on board vessel; and the master of an Army chartered transport or tug is not required in a foreign port to discharge or ship its crew before a consular officer. 230.821 (Opinion of the Judge Advocate General of the Army) Feb 28, 1919."

[DIGEST OF OPINIONS OF THE JUDGE ADVOCATE GENERAL OF THE ARMY, 1912-1940, U. S. Govt. Print. Off, 1942.]

The power to bind a Civil Service seaman to a vessel or other post, or arrest him for desertion from that ship or post was was made under Military Law. (Later in this Appendix, that point will be discussed in detail.)

Criminal Code

The criminal code concerning crimes committed on

the high seas applies to Civil Service seamen as it does
to any other civilian as well as to military personnel.

Coast Guard Discipline Over Civil Service Seamen

The disciplinary power the Coast Guard exercised
over merchant seamen after February 28, 1942, was
duplicated in the case of the Army's Civil Service
seamen. As a method by which standardization of marine
personnel qualifications could be met, the Army had always
utilized the certificating and licensing system as
administered by the Bureau of Marine Inspection and
Navigation. Following the Coast Guard's take over of that
licensing and certificating function, the Army continued
hiring with the requirement that applicants possess
seamen's documents. Therefore, as a practical matter,
suspension or revocation of seamen's documents by the
Coast Guard could ban a seaman from further employment on
Army vessels. The Army cooperated with the Coast Guard in
referring disciplinary cases whenever it was believed that
action should be taken against a seamen's license or
certificate.

Military Discipline: Seamen on Military Auxiliaries

Military law as it applied to World War II was taken from the ARTICLES OF WAR as enacted by the Congress.

"Military law is due process of law to those in the military service of the United States. (Reaves v Ainsworth, 219 US 296 and U.S. ex rel French v Weeks, 259 U.S. 326)."

ARTICLES OF WAR

"Article 2, Persons Subject to Military Law...

"d)   All retainers to the camp and all persons accompanying or serving with the Armies of the United States without the territorial jurisdiction of the United States and in time of war, all such retainees and persons accompanying or serving with the Armies of the United States in the field, both within and without the territorial jurisdiction of the United States although not otherwise subject to these articles;...."

The OPINIONS OF THE JUDGE ADVOCATE OF THE ARMY, published in 1942 makes clear the status of crewmembers of Army vessels.

"(11) ...In time of war, all persons in any manner employed on or serving with chartered transports or transports otherwise in the service or under the control of the Quartermaster's Department of the United States Army are persons 'serving with the armies of the United States in the field,' and are amenable to military law. When seamen enter into contracts to render service on such transports for a specified period, the Government has the right to rely upon them for the performance of their obligation, and if they leave their place of duty with intent to escape service for which they have engaged, they may be arrested as deserters, tried by general court-martial, and punished as prescribed by the Articles of War. (251, Feb 5, 1918.)
      "Crews of Army transports and Army tugs signed on under shipping articles containing "Army clauses" may be arrested and confined by the provost marshal upon the authority of the master of such vessels. The nature of

the duties actually performed by these men, and which
under these "Army clauses" they undertook to perform,
brings them within the scope of the Articles of War and
subjects them to the control of the Army both as to
discipline and punishment and as to the means and methods
of enforcing the same. The master is warranted in causing
the arrest and confinement by the Articles of War and the
Army Transport Service Regulations, Spec. Reg. No. 71,
1917, to which the crew have voluntarily submitted
themselves; and it is his duty, in a proper case, to cause
such arrest and confinement....In time of war when mine
planters are engaged in active service, civilian employees
on such mine planters, like civilian employees on Army
transports, are subject to military law, being persons who
in time of war are serving with the armies of the United
States in the field. A. W. 2 (d). The words 'in the
field,' do not refer to land only but to any place,
whether on land or water, apart from permanent cantonments
or fortifications, where military operations are being
conducted (Ex parte Gerlach, 247 Fed. 616). 250.4, May
31, 1918."

[DIGEST OF OPINIONS OF THE JUDGE ADVOCATE OF THE ARMY
1912-1940, Page 166.]

"Under former section 1473 of this title, a civilian
employed in time of war by Quartermaster's Department and
assigned as cook on a vessel transporting Army supplies
was "serving with the armies in field," and court-martial
had jurisdiction to try him for his attempt to desert the
ship just before sailing. Ex parte Falls, D.C.N.J. 1918,
251 F. 415." [Note 71, Title 10 §802, USCA]

For crewmen on Army transports, the authority of

the Army to impose discipline under military law seems to

have been all inclusive of the seaman's occupational

life. The basis of discipline under military law started

when the Army seaman was within a Port of Embarkation

(POE); it continued while aboard ship; while overseas; and

upon his return to the U. S. until such time that he

individually departed from the confines of a POE. The

United States Fleet instructions as signed by Admiral H.
R. Stark and dated June 8, 1943, previously reproduced in
this Appendix make it clear under 1) (b) of that
document: all discipline concerning Army Transport crews
was considered as "being exclusively under the
jurisdiction of the Army."

> Note: Paragraph 1) (f) of that document is only
> applicable to merchant seamen and not to Civil
> Service seamen employed aboard military
> transports since Army seamen were not the
> responsibility of either the War Shipping
> Administration or the U. S. Consular Service.

Navy Control

Whenever an Army vessel was under Naval routing,
either in convoy or alone, her master was under the
routing and convoy orders of Naval authority. On Army
vessels on which Naval Armed Guards were assigned,
whenever a ship's master assigned crewmembers to gunnery
stations, then while those crewmembers were actually at
such gun stations, they were temporarily under the command
of the Naval gunnery officer and were thus subject to his
orders and discipline. Should a master or crewmember
violate Naval orders in some way, then upon charges to
that effect as lodged by the applicable Naval command, the
Army was the authority through which court martial
proceedings were to be instituted.

[Sailing Orders No. 147, addressed to Master USAT CRISTOBAL, dated February 28, 1943, par 4 (Ship File, Files of Chief of Transportation, Modern Military Records Center, National Archives, Washington.)]
* * * * * *

"Army Regulations   War Department,
    No. 55-330   Washington, December 1, 1942
                        TRANSPORTATION CORPS
    Relationship Aboard Transports of Transport Commander,
            Unit Commanders, Masters, and Others
' * * *.
    ' 5. Provision for and status of Armed Guards.--
    ' (a) Where Navy armed guards are assigned to Army transports, their status and the relationship of their commander to the master will be as prescribed in the appropriate Navy Department regulations governing the assignment of Armed Guards to merchant vessels, as amended from time to time. Neither the transport commander nor the Unit commanders aboard will exercise any command over such guards.
    ' (b) The transport commander and Unit commanders aboard will, at the request of the master, organize details of troops with machine guns and rifles or other available weapons to stand watch, if necessary, and assist in the defense of the ship when called upon to do so, and will cause such drills and exercises of these details to be held as are required to make them proficient in quickly manning stations and opening an effective fire; but the fire of any such weapons will at all times be under the exclusive control of the person charged by the governing regulations with the control of the fire of the permanent armament aboard. Where the permanent Armed Guard is military personnel this will be the master.
    * * *."

[GENERAL INSTRUCTIONS FOR COMMANDING OFFICERS OF NAVAL ARMED GUARDS ON MERCHANT SHIPS, 1943, Third Edition. Navy Department, April 26, 1943.]

COMMENTARY NOTES: APPENDIX B

1   Forfeiture of pay was allowed in one instance under Article of War 104: In time of war or grave national emergency an officer of a grade not less than Brigadier General could impose a fine of not more than one-half month's pay upon a commissioned officer in his command -- but this pertained only to those officers of grades below the rank of major. Following World War II, the Articles of War were replaced by the Uniform Code of Military Justice. Since this study applies only to the World War II period, all references to Military Law refer to the Army's Articles of War and the Navy's Articles for the Government of the U. S. Navy as administered by the Navy through a system of Courts and Boards.

2   In reality, the penalty of confiscation of wages only applied to half of the actual wages earned since by law the seaman could, when in a port, request 50% of his wages in the form of a "draw" against the wages due; thus when contemplating desertion, he would, in all probability, have half of his due wages in pocket. [Title 46, §597, USCA]

3   The Inspectors of the Bureau of Marine Inspection and Navigation were, in 1942, themselves militarized, being commissioned either into the regular Coast Guard or the Coast Guard Reserve.

4   During World War II, contractual language of the shipping articles used by the Army was similar to that used by the War Shipping Administration for merchant seamen, ie., from a certain port, "thence to such ports and places in any part of the world as the Master may direct or as may be ordered or directed by the War Department or [any other authorized agency]." Term of service, "for a voyage not to exceed 12 calendar months."

5   Reference to this contractual arrangement is to be found within the testimony of Col. Alexander Corey who, representing the Transportation Corps, U.S. Army, described same before the Congressional Committee during Hearings of the Committee on Merchant Marine and Fisheries, House of Representatives, 79th Congress, First Session. According to Colonel Corey (page 299 of testimony), such a contract form involved "700 men perhaps." Later (page 302), Colonel Corey states that there were "250 or 300" of such men. [Hearings on H.R. 2346; November 29, 30, December 4, 5, 1945: House of Representatives.]

APPENDIX C

PUBLIC VESSELS ENGAGED IN THE CARRIAGE

OF   COMMERCIAL COMMODITIES

The subject of this Appendix concerns those cases
wherein certain public vessels which were operated by the
military were diverted to carry commercial type goods or
commoditites.

Following World War I, a considerable history of
international litigation developed which delineated those
circumstances by which a "public ship" (or "public
vessel") could lose its sovereign immunity, becoming, by
the nature of its employment, a commercial carrier. As it
turns out, the carriage of commercial cargoes by "public
ships" was a relatively common practice between the two
world wars and even throughout World War II. When engaged
in this kind of activity, are such ships still "public
vessels of a military force?" Or do they, by the test of
their change in use, become merchant vessels?

In the years before World War II, publicly owned
vessels--other than naval fighting ships--were owned and

operated by a number of federal agencies:

The Coast Guard, then under the Treasury Department, had a sizeable fleet which was predominantly concerned with marine safety and enforcement of the Customs Laws.

The Army Corps of Engineers had a fleet engaged in the development and maintenance of harbors and rivers.

The Army's Coast Artillery Corps which operated in cooperation with the Quartermaster Corps, had its own fleet of minelayers and had the attendant responsibility of establishing and maintaining defensive mine fields within harbors and estuaries both in the United States and within its possessions.

The Navy maintained a small number of seagoing cargo ships under the operation of its Naval Transport Service (NTS), a remnant of the large supply force which had been put together by the Navy during World War I.

The Panama Canal Company operated an assortment of passenger/freight vessels which it used in servicing the Canal Zone.

By far the largest operator of "public vessels" was the Army Transport Service (ATS), a sub-agency of the Army's Quartermaster Corps.

Between the wars, servicing American garrisons in the Pacific, became the major task of ATS ships which carried both freight and passengers. In 1938, ATS was running five ships in the Pacific; one other Army Transport was handling Army commitments within the Caribbean.

Although ATS was originally intended to be an auxiliary service solely for the Army, it was asked, at times, to take on added responsibility. For instance, it provided transportation for personnel of the Navy Department or for civilians involved overseas with various federal departments, bureaus, and agencies. To give one such example of how far afield ATS was led:

In the 1930s, upon the joint request of the Departments of Labor and Agriculture, the USAT ST. MIHIEL transported two shiploads of drought stricken farmers from Washington state to Natanuska Valley, Alaska. The authority for this was given in the Act of June 5, 1920, (41 Stat 960; 10 USC 1367) which states that passengers and cargo of a non-military nature could be carried on Army Transports -- provided authority to do so was granted by the Secretary of War. However, such authority to carry non-military personnel and freight was only applicable on a case by case basis -- and then only for emergencies.

[Vessel Letter Files; Files of the Office of the Chief of
Transportation, Modern Military Records Center, National
Archives, Washington, DC.]

     With the outbreak of the war in Europe, various
basic commodities essential to the United States defense
effort came into critical supply. Thus, beginning in
1940, the Government formalized a policy to utilize empty
cargo space on both ATS and NTS operated ships for the
carriage of strategic goods. (Prior to that, these
vessels had oft times made one leg of a voyage carrying
worthless ballast.) Official requests would originate
from the civilian War Production Board's, Stockpiling and
Shipping Division, through its Cargo Forwarding Committee,
and would address either the Army Chief of Staff or, in
the case of the need for a Navy transport, then to the
Chief of Naval Operations (Naval Transport Service). Such
requests were not at all uncommon. The scheduled ATS
voyaging to the Philippines were particularly adaptable in
filling this need as more often than not, a transport
would return from there in at least partial ballast. With
the new need to carry strategic cargo, a transport enroute
back from the Southwest Pacific might would be diverted to
the Dutch East Indies, to take on a cargo of rubber or ore
for the homebound leg. Bulk commoditites were also
regularly carried back by ATS ships engaged on military

supply shuttles to Caribbean bases. For the return trip to the States, a ship might be diverted to load coffee in Columbia or bauxite in British Guiana to be offloaded at a U.S. port.

Similar practices continued after the war started. By such means, the military could better utilize its ships and thus partially overcome the problem of a critical shortage of bottoms. By putting its ships to better use, Army and Navy transportation costs were considerably reduced. There were times, especially during the first year of the war, when strategic cargo was considered to be of even greater priority than direct troop support.

The arrangements through which commodity type cargoes were handled varied. In some cases, a formal time or space charter was undertaken while under other circumstances, the cargo was merely loaded aboard ship and turned over, upon arrival in the U. S., to a responsible federal agency for Governmental sale to an appropriate commercial processor. A formalized arrangement regarding one particular Army Transport is described in Army Transportation Corps files.

In 1942, the Army annex chartered the USAT GIBBINS to the Alcoa Steamship Company.

In format, the "annex charter" was actually a short term form of time (or voyage) charter leaving the Army as the operator of the vessel in all respects.

This was done in response to an urgent request from the U.

S. Maritime Commission. The voyage charter was drawn for

only one leg of the voyage and directed that after the

USAT GIBBINS unloaded Army cargo at Trinidad, it was to

proceed to British Guiana, and load bauxite for return to

a Gulf coast port. Once the bauxite was unloaded, the

annex charter was to terminate. Alcoa -- not the Army --

was the entity actually "engaged in trade." It is

presumed here that Alcoa owned the bauxite, although the

bauxite may have been the temporary property of the United

States War Production Board (a civilian branch of

Government which was not connected with the Army.) In

such a charter, the Army had received compensation for the

temporary use of its vessel's cargo space; thus the public

treasury was enriched, and the total war effort was

benefited since the bauxite was then badly needed for

production of aircraft.

[Vessel name File 9/22/41, QM545.02 T-W-T "Gibbins," correspondence files, Office of Chief of Transportation, Modern Military Records Center, National Archives.]

By entering into an arrangement such as that

which was described, did the USAT GIBBINS temporarily

forfeit her "public vessel" status?

Similar questions have been examined a number of times in the courts and are given in case law as cited on pages 269 through 278 of HANDBOOK OF ADMIRALTY LAW IN THE UNITED STATES by G. H. Robinson, West Publishing Company, 1939. Although not directly answering the exact question of the USAT GIBBINS, these case histories have enough similarity to allow one to draw a conclusion. The points to consider follow:

1. Provided a vessel is owned or operated by the Government, with officers and crew remaining as employees of the Government and with the further circumstance that the ship's activities are directly enriching to the public treasury, then the ship will remain, despite such a voyage charter, as a "public vessel."

2. If governmental operation is conducted by an agency of a nation's armed forces and her crew (military or civilian) is employed by that armed force, then her status in remaining a "public vessel" is even further enhanced.

3. On the other hand, should a vessel which is owned by

an agency of government enter into an arrangement with a corporation, or its agent, under a form of charter so as to effectively engage the vessel in non-governmental management -- such management in turn engaging it in enterprises for private trade and profit -- then that vessel loses her sovereign immunity and with it her status as a "public vessel," becoming, under such circumstances, a merchant vessel by the test of its applied use.

The Army and Navy ships to which this discussion relates clearly retained their "public vessel" status since their activities as commodity carriers were in the direct interest of the Government, and the vessels were continually managed by the Government. Their activity could in no way be connotated with a motivation for private profit (or trade).

COMMENTARY NOTE

The cases which illustrate when a "public vessel" would
lose that status can be readily drawn from World War I,
when certain ships which were requisitioned by the United
States Shipping Board were temporarily time chartered back
to their owners (or Agents) which then utilized them in
trade as conducted for private profit. Those actions
clearly classed those ships as merchant vessels. This
position has been agreed to not only in case law but also
within determinations of the Mixed Claims Commission, an
agency established in 1922 for the administration of war
damage claims directed against Germany. Case histories of
that Commission's decisions are unanimous in establishing
that once ships are removed from the direct management and
purpose of the Government, then their "public vessel"
status no longer applies.

[MIXED   CLAIMS   COMMISSION   (U.   S.   and   Germany)
ADMINISTRATIVE DECISIONS AND OPINIONS OF A GENERAL NATURE,
to   June   30,   1925,   Library   of   Department   of   Justice,
Washington, DC.]

APPENDIX D

CONTEMPORARY STATUS OF MERCHANT SHIPS AND CREWS

SERVING WITH THE ARMED FORCE

(Navy Memorandum 1977)
(Excerpt from Uniform Code of Military Justice)

The following open memorandum, the subject of which is "The Status of Military Sealift Command Vessels," was issued by the Department of State in May of 1977. This memorandum was current as of February 1986 when MERCHANTMAN? OR SHIP OF WAR went to press. It is included here as an Appendix so as to inform the reader that in like manner to World War II, the United States is currently using its merchant ships in the capacity of military auxiliaries and in so doing, how it is imposing upon them both the privileges and the burdens of public vessels in the service of the Armed Forces.

> Note: It is of interest to read in Paragraph 6 that certain vessels serving the Navy in its support force are not so identified; thus, if hostilities broke out tomorrow, merchantmen and auxiliaries would again be indistinguishable from each other.

"SUBJECT: STATUS OF MILITARY SEALIFT COMMAND VESSELS

"Ref: SECSTATE 106685 (1105177 MAY 77)

"1.   Reference (A) Summarized U. S. Government policy
and practice regarding sovereign immunity status of
vessels employed by the U. S. Navy's Military Sealift
Command (MSC).   Recent developments in the Department of
Defense strategic sealift program necessitate a revision
of the policies promligated in Reference (A), which is
hereby cancelled.

"2.   The vessels operated by the MSC are those owned
by the USG, including those in the national defense
reserve fleet; those bareboat chartered to the USG; and
those time or voyage chartered to the USG.   Ships
designated United States Naval Ships (USNS) are either
owned by or bareboat chartered to the US Navy.   MSC
bareboat chartered vessels are privately owned and are
manned either by U. S. Government Civil Service crews or
by contractor employees.   The physical appearance of
bareboat chartered ships either by painting or by stack
markings, is usually the same as U. S. Government owned
USNS.   Privately owned and operated vessels chartered by
MSC for a period of time or for a specified voyage or
voyages are usually manned by civilian private sector
crews employed by a commercial operator, under the
direction of the United States and used exclusively to
transport U. S. Government non-commercial cargo.   They do
not, however, bear distinctive U. S. Government markings.

"3.   Under customary International Law, all vessels
owned or operated by a state and used on government
non-commercial service are entitled to sovereign
immunity.   This means such vessels are, inter alia, immune
from arrest and search, whether in foreign international
or territorial waters or on the high seas: immune from
all foreign taxation; exempt from any foreign state
regulation requiring flying the flag of such foreign state
either in its ports or while passing through its
territorial sea; and entitled to exclusive control over
persons on board such vessels with respect to acts
performed on board.   These ships, however, are expected to
comply voluntarily with the laws of the host state with
regard to order in the ports.   Casting anchor, sanitation
and quarantine, etc.   All vessels in the service of MSC,
whether USG owned, bareboat chartered, time or voyage
chartered, are in exclusive government non-commercial

service. Each of these vessels is entitled to full sovereign immunity.

"4.   In the past, full sovereign immunity has been claimed (and has generally been accorded) for USNS vessels only. As a matter of policy the USG did not claim full sovereign immune status for time and voyage chartered vessels although as a juridical matter our position has been that such vessels are entitled to full immunity. This was done principally to avoid numerous requests for diplomatic clearance and to avoid confusion by foreign states when those vessels entered their ports. With few exceptions, immunitites claimed for such vessels have been limited to freedom from arrest and immunity from taxation, and have been arranged on a bilateral basis.

"5.   For the last few years, MSC has been bringing on line the afloat prepositioning force (APF), most of which is time chartered. In the case of the APF, the policy noted above is not satisfactory. APF vessels are loaded entirely with combat equipment, fuel and combat support supplies. The contents of their cargo is therefore sensitive and cannot be made available for inspection by foreign authorities. APF ships are expected to call only at a limited number of ports and not to make port calls as frequently as e.g., tankers, or general purpose dry cargo carriers. In view of the unique nature of the afloat prepositioning force, it is the policy of the USG that all afloat prepositioning force vessels, including time chartered vessels, must be afforded the full sovereign privileges and immunities currently claimed for and accorded USNS vessels. With respect to MSC voyage chartered vessels and MSC time chartered vessels not a part of the afloat prepositioning force, USG general policy is to continue to claim immunity only from arrest and taxation. Circumstances may arise which necessitate assertions of sovereign immunity for time or voyage chartered vessels in addition to those in the APF. When such cases have arisen in the past, specific guidance has been provided at the time. This procedure will continue.

"6.   Request all posts take appropriate action to insure host governments are aware, when appropriate, of the status of sovereign immune vessels and assist in assuring recognition of this status. Posts should be aware that afloat prepositioning force time chartered MSC ships will require diplomatic clearance for port calls in foreign countries. The request for diplomatic clerance will explicitly identify these vessels as afloat prepositioning force ships of MSC. They may not be painted distinctively or bear the MSC logo. It is essential for posts to impress upon their host governments the status of such ships in the event of port calls or other operations in host government territorial seas and internal waters. The list of ships currently in the APS is available from the Chief of Naval Operations (OP-42). ARMACOST BT"

* * * *

"CHAPTER 47, UNIFORM CODE OF MILITARY JUSTICE

"Article 2, Persons subject to the chapter

   "(a) The following persons are subject to this chapter:

      "(10) In times of war, persons serving with or accompanying an armed force in the field."

[Title 10 §802, USCA]

APPENDIX E

PUBLIC LAW 95-202

In 1977, the Congress passed Public Law 95-202
which allows benefits under statutes administered by the
Veterans Administration. P.L. 95-202 was created for
civilian groups whose service could be considered
"equivalent to active military service." Applications for
approval under P.L. 95-202 are administered by the
Department of Defense (Office of the Secretary of the Air
Force) by its Civilian/Military Review Board.

The merchant marine of World War II (Contested
Waters Group), a comprehensive applicant group, was denied
approval in October 1985, on the grounds that its service,
as a group, was "too global and too diversified"
[organizationally] to be considered as one comprehensive
group (Civilian/Military Review Board ruling). 1   The
author of the "Contested Waters Group" application did not
present the evidence in the legally encompassing way it
has been treated here within MERCHANTMAN? OR SHIP OF WAR.
Since the enactment of P.L. 95-202 in 1977, several

applications (in addition to the "Contested Waters Group" application) have been filed under the law on behalf of civilian seamen; however none of the applications have had, as their basis of argument, the wording that the oceangoing merchant marine of World War II was actually "a part of the United States Armed Forces." 2 Those words, if properly argued, would, in my opinion, have been the defensible key to merchant marine group acceptance under P.L. 95-202.

COMMENTARY NOTES: APPENDIX E

1   The Contested Waters Group encompassed four subgroups:

a)   Seamen on Army ships
b)   Seamen on merchant ships allocated to the military
c)   Seamen on merchant ships which carried, in some part,
     military consigned cargo
d)   Seamen on merchant ships which were engaged in the carriage
     of military lend-lease cargoes.

By its generalized description, the "Contested Waters Group" enfolded other merchant marine groups which were also at the time being reviewed under P.L. 95-202. These were the "Invasion Group" and the "Mulberry Group."

All of the above were rejected as eligible under P.L. 95-202 under the earlier stated primary reasoning.

In 1980, a group known as "Merchant Marine in Ocean Service in WW II" was rejected. In 1979, a group identified as "Army Crewmen, WW II" was also turned down. Both of those disapprovals were made primarily on the basis that the Review Board believed that the groups, as legally described within the applications, did not meet the criteria of the enabling law.

Three groups which in whole or part contained civilian seamen have been approved:

1980:   "Civilian Employees, Defenders of Wake Island." (This group included approximately half a dozen civilian seamen who were employed aboard a tug at the time of the surrender of Wake Island to the Japanese.)

1984:   "HENRY KESWICK Group, Corregidor." (These were seamen employed by the Army during the defensive phase Bataan/Corregidor, 1941-42.)

1985:   "Blockship Group." (Merchant seamen employed by the War Shipping Administration aboard ships which were scuttled for a breakwater off the Normandy Beachhead, June 1944.)

2   Applications for the merchant marine per se do not properly describe Civil Service seamen who served on military auxiliary vessels belonging to the Army or Navy since such groups are not legally encompassed under the term "merchant marine." Application under P.L. 95-202 for Army or Navy seamen should, in the future, be handled as completely separate entities.

BIBLIOGRAPHY

BOOKS

Allen, Gardner W. OUR NAVAL WAR WITH FRANCE, by Houghton Mifflin Company, Boston and New York 1909.]

Bes, J. CHARTERING AND SHIPPING TERMS, Fourth Edition. Amsterdam: 1956.

BLACKS LAW DICTIONARY, Revised Fourth Edition, West Publishing Company: 1968.

BRITISH VESSELS LOST AT SEA 1914-18. Patrick Stephens, Cambridge, England: 1977. (Reprint of NAVY LOSSES AND MERCHANT SHIPPING LOSSES, His Majesty's Stationery Office, London: 1919)

Brittin, Burdick H. INTERNATIONAL LAW FOR SEAGOING OFFICERS, 4th Edition. Naval Institute Press, Annapolis, MD: 1981

Chatterton, Kebel. Q-SHIPS AND THEIR STORY. Naval Institute Press, Annapolis, MD: 1972.

Clephane, Lewis P., with Naval History Division. HISTORY OF THE NAVAL OVERSEAS TRANSPORTATION SERVICE IN WORLD WAR I. Naval History Division, Department of the Navy. Washington: 1969

Davidson, Eugene. THE TRIALS OF THE GERMANS, NUREMBERG, 1945-1946. The MacMillan Company. New York: 1966.

DICTIONARY OF AMERICAN FIGHTING SHIPS, Volume II. Naval History Division, Department of the Navy. Washington: 1963

Hohman, Elmo Paul. THE HISTORY OF AMERICAN MERCHANT SEAMEN. Shoe String Press. Hamden, Connecticut: 1956.

Hurley, Edward N. THE BRIDGE TO FRANCE. J. B. Lippincott Company, Philadelphia, 1927.

Meilach, Jordan. BELL BOTTOM SHORTS. Carlton Press. New York: 1968.

MERCHANT VESSELS OF THE UNITED STATES, U. S. Department of Commerce. Government Printing Office, Washington: 1917; 1918; 1919; and 1920.

Moore, Arthur R. A CARELESS WORD...A NEEDLESS SINKING. United States Merchant Marine Academy Museum, Kings Point, NY: 1983.

Morison, Samuel Eliot. THE BATTLE OF THE ATLANTIC: U.S. NAVAL OPERATIONS IN WW II, Volume I. Atlantic Little Brown. Boston: 1970.

Noel, John V. and Edward L. Beach. NAVAL TERMS DICTIONARY. 4th Edition. Naval Institute Press. Annapolis, MD: 1978

Reisenberg, Felix. SEA WAR, Reinhart and Company, Inc.. New York: 1956.

Rene deKerchove, compiler. INTERNATIONAL MARITIME DICTIONARY, Second Edition. Van Nostrand Reinhold, New York, London, 1961.

Risch, Erna. QUARTERMASTER SUPPORT OF THE ARMY, A HISTORY OF THE CORPS, 1775-1939. Quartermaster's Historians Office, Office of the Quartermaster General. Washington, DC: 1962.

Safford, Jeffrey J. AMERICA'S MARITIME LEGACY: A HISTORY OF THE U. S. MERCHANT MARINE AND SHIPPING INDUSTRY SINCE COLONIAL TIMES. Westview Press: 1979.

Savage, Carlton. POLICY OF THE UNITED STATES TOWARD MARITIME COMMERCE IN WAR, Volume I, 1776-1914, Department of State. Government Printing Office. Washington, DC: 1934.

Savage, Carlton. POLICY OF THE UNITED STATES TOWARD MARITIME COMMERCE IN WAR, Volume II, 1914-1918, Department of State. Government Printing Office. Washington, DC: 1936.

Scharf, J. Thomas. HISTORY OF THE CONFEDERATE STATES NAVY, Fairfax Press (reprint), New York: 1977

THE AMERICAN HERITAGE DICTIONARY OF THE ENGLISH LANGUAGE. Houghton Mifflin Company. Boston and New York: 1969

THE MURDER OF CAPTAIN FRYATT. Hodder and Stoughton. London and New York: 1916

Turpin, Edward A. and William A. MacEwen. MERCHANT MARINE OFFICERS HANDBOOK, Cornell Maritime Press. New York: 1943.

Wardlow, Chester. U. S. ARMY IN WORLD WAR II, The Technical Series, Transportation Corps Responsibilities, Organization, and Operation. Office of the Chief of Military History. U.S. Government Printing Office. Washington: 1951.

JOURNALS AND MISCELLANEOUS GOVERNMENT PUBLICATIONS

BRITISH AND FOREIGN MERCHANT VESSELS LOST OR DAMAGED BY ENEMY ACTION DURING SECOND WORLD WAR, 3 September 1939 to 2 September 1945, BR 1337, Naval Staff (Trade Division), British Admiralty

DIGEST OF OPINIONS OF THE JUDGE ADVOCATE GENERAL OF THE ARMY, 1912-1940. U.S. Government Printing Office. Washington: 1942

Goertner, Francis B. HISTORY OF THE MARITIME WAR EMERGENCY BOARD, Prepared for the United States Department of Labor: Washington, 1950

Hackworth, Green Haywood. DIGEST OF INTERNATIONAL LAW, Volume VI, Chapters XIX-XXI. Department of State. U.S. Government Printing Office. Washington: 1943.

HOUSE HEARINGS; MERCHANT MARINE AND FISHERS COMMITTEE. 79th Congress, October 18, 1945 (H H-MER 16), pp 1-274), New York Law Institute

INTERNATIONAL LAW SITUATIONS, 1930. Naval War College. Government Printing Office, Washington: 1931.

LAW OF NAVAL WARFARE, NWIP 10-2. Office of the Chief of Naval Operations, Department of Navy. Washington: 1955

Mallison, W. T., Jr. INTERNATIONAL LAW STUDIES, Volume LVIII, NAVPERS 15031. Naval War College, Newport, Rhode Island: 1966.

MIXED CLAIMS COMMISSION (U. S. AND GERMANY) ADMINISTRATIVE DECISIONS AND OPINIONS OF A GENERAL NATURE, October 1926 to December 1932. Department of Justice. Washington, DC.

MIXED CLAIMS COMMISSION (U. S. AND GERMANY) ADMINISTRATIVE DECISIONS AND OPINIONS OF A GENERAL NATURE, TO JUNE 30, 1925. Department of Justice. Washington, DC.

"The Declaration of Paris in Modern War," LAW QUARTERLY REVIEW, Vol 55. London: 1939.

WAR INSTRUCTIONS FOR UNITED STATES MERCHANT VESSELS (C.S.P. 131), January 1918. Navy Department, U.S. Government Printing Office, Washington: 1918.

Whiteman, Marjorie M. DIGEST OF INTERNATIONAL LAW, Volume X. Department of State. U.S. Government Printing Office. Washington.

UNPUBLISHED DOCUMENTS AND MONOGRAPHS

Conference Series No. 6, 1931. London Naval Conference of 1930. Department of State

Cumulative Supplement to the Code of Federal Regulations of the United States of America; Title 33 in Title 45; Title 34--Navy, Chapter I; Department of the Navy. Divison of the Federal Register. U. S. Government Printing Office. Washington: 1944.

Department of State File No. 763.72/2636a.

Department of State File No. 763.72111/226a; 1914.

FF1/A14-1, Serial 6077; 25 Dec. 1942. Navy Department Bulletin; Cumulative Edition. Navy Department: December 31, 1943.

Foreign Relations, U. S. Supplement 245 246, 1916: 1929

GENERAL INSTRUCTIONS FOR COMMANDING OFFICERS OF NAVAL ARMED GUARD ON MERCHANT SHIPS, (OPNAV 23L-2) 4th Edition. Navy Department: 1944.

HISTORY OF THE ARMING OF MERCHANT SHIPS AND THE NAVAL ARMED GUARD SERVICE (an unpublished study on microfilm). Division of Naval History, Department of Navy. Washington, DC.

Memorandum to Asst. Secretary of the Navy Bard, signed R. R. Waesche, Vice Admiral, USCG: 13 July 1943

Memorandum to Masters of all Merchant Vessels, 31 December 1942; P 13-9 (34073-14-B/Sk.) Signed by J.W. Greenslade, Navy Department.

Mr. Larson's Files: Ship files; Second Drawer, Cabinet 16, Stack No. 3, National Records Center. National Archives, Suitland, Maryland.

Operations Regulations No. 35. War Shipping Administration: January 25, 1943.

QM545.02 T-W-T "Gibbins," Correspondence File, Vessel Name Files; Files of the Office of Chief of Transportation. Modern Military Records Center. National Archives.

Redistribution of Maritime Functions. Executive Order No. 9083: Effective February 28, 1942.

Sailing Orders No. 147, addressed to Master of USAT CRISTOBAL, dated February 28, 1943. Ship Files; Files of Chief of Transportation. Modern Military Records Center. National Archives.

UNITED STATES NAVAL VESSELS LOST DURING THE WAR (WW II). Navy Department: 2 October 1945.

Vessel Crewing Files (Information File), Office Chief of Transportation Files, Modern Military Records Center. National Archives

Vessel Letter Files; Files of Chief of Transportation. Modern Military Records Center. National Archives.

Washington Conference #274. Senate Document No. 126, 67th Congress, 2nd Session: 1922

INDEX

Notes

Notes

Notes

Notes

Notes

Notes